TALES OF MAIN STREET, VANCOUVER, BC

Tales of Main Street, Vancouver, BC

KG Dennis

Copyright © 2012, MMHC Ltd.

All rights reserved. No part of this book may be reproduced, stored, or transmitted by any means—whether auditory, graphic, mechanical, or electronic—without written permission of both publisher and author, except in the case of brief excerpts used in critical articles and reviews. Unauthorized reproduction of any part of this work is illegal and is punishable by law.

ISBN 978-0-9879752-1-8

Preface

Dear Friends and Community of Main Street, Everywhere

This book is a Latte Book. It is the cost of a coffee, made with organic beans from faraway farmers happy to be in a fair trade agreement, and can be read while drinking the coffee in a café on Main Street. Enjoy.

The time has come for me to rest my weary head, now with gray hair, and put my feet up by the fire to spin shaggydogs about how we used to have to walk miles, not kilometres, to and from a new chain store at a new mall, through daily sub-zero white-out blizzards, before global warming/climate change, to buy bread that cost a dime a loaf, and needed to be enriched with four artificial vitamins – over on Main Street in Vancouver, BC, Canada.

Come join me for a tale or two.
Cheers,
KG Dennis
December 21, 2011

Disclaimer

In the words of the great Canadian storyteller, Stephen Leacock, in his famous book, *Sunshine Sketches of a Little Town*:

"Personally, I would sooner have written "Alice in Wonderland" than the whole Encyclopaedia Britannica."

Like Leacock's 'Mariposa,' Main Street, Vancouver could be considered Main Street, Everywhere. There are some general descriptions of the Main Street, Vancouver that I love, but it is the Main Street of my imagination that I write of.

- KGD

Contents

Preface v
1. Main Street Against the War on Drugs 1
2. The Dogs of Main Street 17
3. Mountain View Madness 27
4. Main Street Mudras 37
5. Main Street Mining 53
6. Murder on Main Street 65
7. Women Watching on Main Street 75

Main Street Against the WOD

Main Street in Vancouver, B.C. goes from the Burrard Inlet up and over a huge hill down to the mighty Fraser River. From the top of the hill looking west, you can see the Salish Sea, the Georgia Strait and sometimes an island; to the north, the sky frames the North Shore mountains; to the east, lie Grouse Mountain and Burnaby Mountain; and far off in the distance, up in the clouds to the south, Mt. Baker, in Washington, USA reveals its snowy peak on a sunny day.

On the hill, looking south towards the river, you can see the Fraser estuary spreading out before you, a massive delta where only man, in his questionable wisdom, would build an airport. Beyond the delta to the southwest, lies Point Roberts, and due south, the Peace Arch straddles B.C.'s southern border.

The hill that Main Street straddles is called South Hill, as is the neighbourhood that faces south towards the Fraser River. South Hill has nice homes with well-tended yards; some have spectacular gardens with gorgeous, semi-tropical rainforest plants with big leaves as a lush canopy. On this hill, one hundred years ago, stood an ancient forest, a grove of beautiful, towering cedar trees thousands of years old. Such primeval beauty was never to be seen again, thanks to the industrious zeal of our forefathers to develop land. They didn't leave one single tree. The oldest trees now are perhaps fifty years old. Two of them stand side-by-side in front of two homes in South Hill. One house is wooden, painted white with blue trim. The other is grey stucco with green trim, both houses from the building boom of the fifties.

Living in these homes back in the nineties were two families that had been neighbours since they were both young couples starting out. Nirmala and Bukajeet had gone on to have three girls, a cause of complaint for Bukajeet who was given to drunken ranting about not having a son. They had even brought over a nephew from the mother country to adopt as a son. Though tradition was satisfied, his drunken tirades were not.

Susan and Mark, next door, had never been blessed with any children. They had tried when they were young to no avail, moving on to live content lives, happy with each other, serenely accepting whatever life brought or didn't bring. Susan poured her heart into her garden. Every flower was a child, every tree a relative. She had adopted a large family of plants that she tended with all of the love in her heart. When she was puttering in her garden, she hummed with pleasure. Mark loved Susan's garden too, because he loved her. They both loved Ralph, a golden retriever. Back when Ralph was young, before arthritis set in, he and Mark had been volunteers with Search and Rescue, enjoying many an hour working as a team.

Both women were avid gardeners. They'd spent many hours chatting through many seasons as they moved about tending their plants, Susan with her flowers, Nirmala with her vegetables and herbs. Both women, in flip-flops, baggy shirts and pants, were holding trowels in their flowered-cotton-gloved hands, their heads covered by wide-brimmed hats. Susan leaned towards Maiwa from Granville Island, even Carole Little or Laura Ashley from Bellis Fair. Nirmala always wore traditional clothes in beautiful fabrics of stunning colours.

Standing at the old chain-link fence, Susan and Nirmala were involved in one of their more serious conversations.

"What am I supposed to do?" said Nirmala. She was shaking her trowel up and down, a magic wand banishing evil.

"I don't know," replied Susan. "What a horrible thing to have to deal with."

"He doesn't listen to me." She rubbed at the tears dribbling down her cheeks, smearing a line of dirt across her face. "He was such a good boy." The thought of what was lost brought on another spasm. She choked on her pain, her hands covering her broken heart, her head bowed, her tears soaking the soil beneath her feet. She wept for the boy, Gurlochan, brought over when he was fourteen to be Bukajeet's son. He'd been a fresh-faced innocent then, just in from a village in the countryside, barely speaking English. Off he'd gone to John Oliver Secondary School, full of optimism for the fabulous doors opening up before him.

It was spring then. Nirmala was planting cilantro, peppers, spinach, potatoes, carrots, and some roses. Susan was putting in a pond so that she could grow lilies and have real frogs. She'd had enough of frog knick-knacks. She was going to raise tadpoles to hear the sound of frogs at night in the summer time, like it used to be. There had always been frogs croaking at night in the sultry summers, then they'd gone away. No more tadpoles in the ponds: only more suburban housing. Susan was digging a beautiful pond to bring back frogs. She'd dug one at the bottom of the garden before thinking that it would be better in the top corner, so she was filling in the old hole before digging anew.

Susan was leaning on her spade next to their fence. "You need tough love. If he's going to run with gangs, get loaded, and basically drop out of school, you have to tell him he has to find his own place to live or else go into treatment. Give him a choice. You must keep you and your girls safe. He needs to know that your home is a sanctuary, not part of his gang world, and as long as he's in a gang, he can't live with you. It sounds harsh, but you have to hold the line."

"I can't do that. Where would he go? We're responsible for him. And my home is not a sanctuary. Look at Bukajeet. They hate each other. Bukajeet never stops yelling at him."

They both stood still. Oh yes, Bukajeet as a role model, happily drinking his life away, except for when he was terrorizing his wife and children with rants and rages. He was trapped in an arranged marriage to a woman who'd borne only girls, no boys. Only alcohol understood his woe. "If Gurlochan is into hard drugs, he's not who you think he is anymore," said Susan. "Think of it like this: a demon is absorbing his spirit and you're in mortal combat with a monster."

Nirmala dropped her trowel, pulled off her flowered gloves, and took the tissue that Susan offered.

"It's those drugs," said Susan. "The refined ones that look like white powders are the problem. They're all highly addictive.

No one has ever seen them before. We're all flying by the seat of our pants. What are parents supposed to do?"

"You're right," said Nirmala. "No one can cope with the craziness of these drugs. How can it be allowed? How can this be happening? What crazy people make them?"

Talking about her problems calmed Nirmala. After falling in with the wrong high-school crowd, her adopted son had taken to wearing striped Ali-Baba pants, a white wife-beater T-shirt, gold necklaces, and bracelets, slicked back hair, and a goatee of sorts. He looked spruced up, like he was stepping out of Disney's *Aladdin* movie, but he saw himself as an action-film hero, carrying weapons to shoot enemies, making off with loot to enjoy a fun-filled life of best buddies, fast girls, and high times, especially when they were loaded.

This was three months before the shooting.

The gang that Gurlochan joined called themselves the Los Diablos. This particular summer, in the early-1990s, someone's family had bought the pizza place at Main and 41st in delusional desperation, hoping that work would knock some sense into their son. Instead, the plaza filled up every night with a crowd of young men wearing striped Ali-Baba pants and white wife-beater T-shirts, just like Gurlochan. They drove expensive cars, shiny and new, and swaggered about with youthful oblivion.

The Penny Lane pub was in the same plaza as the pizza place. All summer long, when the pub closed, the sounds of violence filled the air as the youth rolled drunks and fought each other. "Kill him, kill him," could be heard echoing up Woodstock Avenue, leaving the neighbours in fear for their lives. The police were useless. By the time they arrived, the boys were scattered, the deadly game evaporated.

One hot, humid night in the middle of a heat wave, Susan had stepped outside at 3 a.m. in the moonlight, unable to sleep. Gurlochan was sitting on the steps of the porch next door, smoking a cigarette. She turned when she noticed him and said hello. He said hello back. Then he got up and walked over, asking if she knew what time it was, which she did only too well. He told her that he had lost his keys. Susan could tell that he was stoned but lucid, not slurring his words. He was exuding a meditative air, as if sitting on the steps after locking himself out had made a dint in the delusions that he had been trying to live out.

Gurlochan began to confide in her, like Susan was his auntie whom he could say anything to.

"I have to get away from that high school," he said. "It's not good. I'll never get anywhere if I stay there." He shook his head from side to side, his face creased with worry. "That school is bad."

He was talking about John Oliver, at 41st and Fraser, across from Mountain View Cemetery, named after one of the premiers of the province, one of B.C.'s founding fathers. Gurlochan couldn't have cared less. He'd parachuted into a Vancouver high school, no different than any other one in North America, chocked to the rafters with the drug business. He'd buddied up with guys who spoke his language, only to find himself hanging around in private family rooms in huge, brand-new houses getting drunk and stoned, watching violent, sexy stuff on TV, playing with guns, and driving around in cool cars.

Gurlochan told Susan all of this and that he was tired of the lifestyle. He wanted to get an education and a good job. He didn't want to be involved in all of the insane things that the guys were doing. He needed to get away from them. He asked her how he could do that. She told him to take a trade at a different school, become an apprentice, hang out with older men doing good work.

This was six weeks before the shooting.

"You should make Gurlochan take an apprenticeship program to give him some direction," said Susan. "Get him away from those boys he hangs around with."

Nirmala and Susan were busy in their gardens on a fine, soft, summer evening. A gentle breeze was coming off the Pacific Ocean. The sun, setting slowly, cast a deepening, warm, golden glow onto their little patches of earth. Susan was deadheading her flowerbeds while on the lookout for signs of morning glory and buttercups. Nirmala was cutting from a huge patch of mustard plants.

"Bukajeet won't let him," she replied. Gurlochan had broached the idea. A failure. Bukajeet wanted to send him back to the mother country. It was a no-go.

"Send him to a different school for some specialized trade," said Susan.

"His grades aren't good enough right now," said Nirmala. That road was a dead end. She'd even gone with Gurlochan to meet with the school vice-principal to see what could be done. Nothing.

"Send him to Total Ed down on Prince Edward Street. It's an alternative school for kids that don't fit into regular school. He'd love it there."

"I'll see what he says. He's so different now, even in the last few weeks. He gets worse every day. It's awful."

Gurlochan was still arriving home in the wee hours in a fancy-schmancy car full of raucous, high-on-gangster-life boys who were drunk or stoned. He would come tumbling out onto the grass boulevard, crawling a few paces as he staggered to his feet, swaying and waving his arms in drunken balance. With a squeal and a pip-pip, the shiny car with the little wheels would roar off down the street, carrying its cargo of youth, thinking that they had it all, that Main Street was their oyster.

Susan could only look at her friend in sympathy. "What a problem to have." They had both stopped all efforts to garden and now stood at the fence. Nirmala held a bunch of mustard, Susan a beautiful rose in full bloom, dark red and scented.

"He made friends with this boy named Razinder. Ever since then, it's been terrible. It's Razzy this and Razzy that all the time. All he talks about is what Razinder wears, Razinder's goatee, his shoes, his car. I asked him what about Razinder's job, what about gangs, why on earth would they call themselves the Los Diablos of all things, what are they thinking of? Have they forgotten where we're from? That shut him up for a minute. I know this Razinder's parents from temple."

Susan could see the black rings around Nirmala's eyes, the kind of black from all-night anxiety attacks, staring at the ceiling, heart-pounding worry, wondering what to do, what best to do, worry and more worry. Her face sagged, her once-cheerful smile was gone, her mouth dragged her cheeks down into jowls. There were new lines on her forehead. The most telling detail was her hair; once bright and shiny, it now hung in dull, dry fluff around her face, an unkempt heap. What Nirmala was this? Susan's heart softened for her friend. She reached out and touched her shoulder. Standing motionless, they looked at each other, finding solace in each other's eyes.

"I want Gurlochan to sleep in the garden shed," said Nirmala. "I'll clean it out, fix it up, put a bed in there so he doesn't wake us up when he comes home. What else can I do?" She was trying to explain to herself as much as to Susan, even to the mustard plants that she had in her hand. Explain the inexplicable. Make it up as you go.

"I can't have him coming and going at all hours, drunk and who knows what. He scares the girls. I have no idea what he does, where he goes. Why are they driving around in those cars? Who pays for them? What are their parents thinking? They're not all millionaires. And Bukajeet. He won't have anything to do with Gurlochan. He pretends he doesn't exist most of the time, but when he drinks, oh my god. He's going to kill him one of these days. It's unbearable. How can they be so stupid? What on earth is wrong with these men? Do other women put up with this? I can't believe it."

"Gurlochan is into drug-dealing in a gang. He's addicted to boot," said Susan. "Never mind the garden shed. You've got to get him into treatment, away from your house, away from everything he knows right now. He needs professional help, not the garden shed." She handed Nirmala the rose.

"How do I get him to treatment when he doesn't want to go? What kind of schools are these? He learned this in school. How can that be?" The distance from a country village, in the middle of the sub-continent of India, to a Main Street high school was shocking.

Nirmala twirled the rose under her nose, breathing in its sweet fragrance. For one blissful moment, she enjoyed life, gardening, and friendship.

This was one month before the shooting.

One morning that summer, Nirmala went to jump into her station wagon but it wasn't there. It eventually showed up. She went down to the Insurance Corporation of B.C. at Cambie and Marine to see what the thief had done to it. Something like a big tree or telephone pole had gone through the front window on the driver's side, smashing the seat to bits. It was hard to believe that anyone could survive such an accident, so the driver must have rolled it down a slope in the woods somewhere.

"It was one of those kids he hangs around with," said Nirmala, "because I said something to Razinder's mother at the temple. All I said was that her son had a very nice car but maybe Gurlochan should just walk home instead of troubling Razinder for a ride. It was nothing, but Gurlochan came home and shouted at me. Why had I talked to Razinder's mother? I was not allowed to talk to her. He was talking like a crazy person."

They had met on the sidewalk in front of their homes under the huge chestnut trees. It was a sunny day, with little flecks of gold filtering in through the deep green leaves high above them. Nirmala was now driving a loaner. She had been out to look at new cars, wondering whether to get another station wagon or something bigger and more comfortable for her and the children. A van maybe.

"Humpf," said Susan. "Not allowed to talk to her. Honestly, these boys. It just shows you what the drug business does to people. She must know."

"Oh, she must and her other children must all know too. Everyone must know by now. Even I know. Who do they think they're kidding? They expect everyone to be as stupid as them."

They both noticed Gurlochan limping along the sidewalk towards them. They waved, calling out a greeting as he approached. The smiles quickly died as they saw how he looked.

"I got in a fight," he said. He looked dazed and bedraggled, not the smart lad at all. His Ali-Baba pants were torn, as was the wife-beater shirt. His coiffed hair stuck out in all directions, still stiff with gel. The gold chains were gone.

"I have to go away," he said. With his face swollen and lip bleeding, he had some trouble speaking up.

"You need to go to the hospital," said Susan. "You need to get stitched up and x-rayed for broken bones."

"No," he said, curling his shoulders in pain. "I can't do that. I have to go away right now and never come back. Help me get away."

Susan looked at Nirmala, who was standing, petrified and speechless. She had no idea what to say or do. She could only stare at Gurlochan in horror.

"Go to the hospital first," Susan said. She tried to look into his eyes. He turned his head away before trying to stand like a person not in acute pain.

"No, no. No hospital. Please, no hospital. I don't want to go," he said.

A car screeched far down the street. They all turned their heads towards the sound, although none of them could see anything. Gurlochan's face jumped with fear, his eyes suddenly darting about, his mouth a grimace of panic. He raised his arms in reflex, as if to ward off an attacker. He moved with surprising speed down the path towards the backyard and quickly disappeared. He didn't have relatives in Flin Flon or Halifax. He didn't know how to disappear up north into the labour camps or south across the border into the multitudes of people in the States. Instead, he lurked around his neighbourhood, playing psychopathic cat and terrified mouse with boys who believed that killing someone ended the game.

Nirmala and Susan stared at the open gate, then looked at each other. What on earth was going on?

This was fifteen days before the shooting.

Susan was shocked. Nirmala had a shiner. A major shiner. Puffy purple and black, it added to the already worn-out-with-worry face she'd been wearing for the last while. It didn't look like things could get worse. Bukajeet and Gurlochan had both gone insane on drugs and alcohol, rage, and shame, in a deadly dance together.

Susan realized that both men, for different reasons, could be violent towards Nirmala, who didn't drink, didn't get loaded or run with gangsters. They thought that she was their victim, below them on the pecking order. Suck up, peck down, they thought in their world of men. Down meant Nirmala, all adult and responsible in her women's world.

They were sitting in Susan's living room. Nirmala had come for tea.

"Bukajeet's still in the hospital," she said. Her lower lip trembled. "He hit me so I hit him back this time on top of his head with the frying pan. He fell down on the kitchen floor so I kicked him." She paused, painfully struggling for words.

"I couldn't stop kicking him. My eldest daughter came in. She kicked him too. The young ones came in. There we were, all kicking him."

She was crying now, but determined to tell Susan how it ended. "When I saw my girls hitting their father, I could only watch. I saw their faces."

She lifted her head, her face raw and vulnerable. "I told them to stop. Then we all hugged and cried and hugged. Then we called an ambulance. We told them he slipped on the floor in his slippers. He was drunk and smelled anyway. They never said anything. They never do. Only we know. But how can I let him come back? I want him to stay at the hospital forever. I don't care if I'm never allowed to go to temple again. He's not coming back here."

"You poor thing," said Susan. "Look at you. What a terrible thing to happen. You must be beside yourself." Susan crossed the room to sit on the couch. She took Nirmala by the shoulders to bring her into a heartfelt hug. "You poor, poor, sweet dear. Don't worry now. The worst is over. He doesn't have to come back. Ever. We'll get you the best lawyer in town, don't you worry. This is something Mark and I can help you with. You'll come out of this on your feet. You and your girls will do just fine on your own. Don't worry." She held Nirmala as tears fell.

"Gurlochan too," said Nirmala. "No more garden shed, no more anything at all. He's not coming back either. I can't take it anymore. He's gone crazy. I'm going to change the locks. He can't come here. He can't bring those boys around. I can't take it anymore."

"Of course not, my dear. It's far too much for anyone. You have your girls to consider. Gurlochan has to come to his own realizations about the life he's leading. Only he can decide not to do drugs. It's not up to you to make his decision. It's up to you to give him a choice. It's his personal responsibility. He has to recognize that he's sick now. He needs to be in treatment. You've done all you can providing a home for him. He has to decide what kind of lifestyle he wants. It's not up to you anymore."

"How can this be happening?" asked Nirmala. Her face was scrunched up in pain. "What kind of choices are these? They're like no choices."

There is a special hell realm for parents with drug-addicted children. Nirmala had fallen down into that pit of horror.

This was ten days before the shooting.

Susan had finally gotten the hole for the pond the right size and shape, and then it rained. Although the hole had turned into a giant mud puddle, all she saw was the frog-friendly ecosystem that she was creating. She thought of how happy her frogs would be, croaking in her pond.

"Oh, life's a quagmire of politics," said Susan. They were seated at the table in Nirmala's kitchen looking out the window at the puddle on the other side of the fence, growing bigger in the rain.

They looked at each other, their lips resting above the delicate china of Nirmala's tea cups. The warm, milky, fragrant tea tasted sweet and soothing. Her kitchen was cozy and clean, organized and loved. It was the hearth of her home, now a sanctuary, her little part of the world. Nirmala had been talking about how people at the temple were responding to her leaving Bukajeet. She had received unexpected sympathy from places she hadn't thought possible.

"I haven't seen Gurlocan," said Nirmala. "I went up to the school but they haven't seen him. I asked that Razinder kid when I saw him with his mother at the Superstore down at Main and Marine. He said he hasn't seen him either but I know he was lying. He looked angry too. What is the matter with that boy?"

"He must know where he is," said Susan.

Nirmala was shaking her head. She truly could not understand what was happening to Gurlochan, a drug dealer and addict. "How can he be in a gang?" she asked, bewildered.

Susan rolled her eyes heavenward, thinking about foreign policy, the CIA and globally integrated drug traffic headed right into our schools, aimed at our children. It is too cynical for words, the international drug business, she thought.

"It goes beyond our neighbourhood, this whole drug business, this war on drugs. It's all over the world. It's a disaster for people in many countries. It doesn't serve us well."

She looked at Nirmala with a twinkle in her eye.

"We need something completely new like The Mothers' Cannabis Distribution Company. We can use all of those billions of dollars to fund real treatment centres for people with mental health problems. We can put money towards things that all children need."

Nirmala laughed. "What silly ideas you have. Can you imagine? We couldn't do that. It would be a terrible thing to do."

"What has happened to Gurlochan is terrible," said Susan.

"Oh, what am I supposed to do? Go out on the streets to look for him? Where? I go to the market, to temple, and home. I have no idea where he could be. Why doesn't he call at least?"

"He hasn't called because he knows you want him to see a doctor and get help. What on earth can you do?"

This was six days before the shooting.

Nirmala and Susan were in their gardens. Nirmala was cutting cilantro while telling Susan how to make green chutney. Susan was mulling over the recipe, trying to figure out how to add some plums from her plum tree.

The gate slammed. They both jumped and turned around to see Gurlochan staggering up the path looking disheveled, unclean, and angry.

"You got me in trouble," he shouted. "It's your fault. You're always getting me in trouble."

He jittered and jumped about. They looked at him twitching, so sorry to see him so sick, so out of it. "I need some money," he mumbled.

Nirmala was frozen in shock. Before she could move, he bounded down the path to the back gate. He vanished again.

Much later, they learned that after he'd left them, he had stolen a purse from a woman in the Punjabi Market. He had mugged her right on Main Street, hitting her and wrestling with her for her purse. Bystanders had almost apprehended him, but he got away; at least, people had recognized him. Now the police were looking for him.

This was four days before the shooting.

Susan was filling her pond. The plastic liner covered the hole. The pump was finally working, the hose didn't leak, and the fountain flowed water. Her vision of water lilies blooming and frogs croaking was that much closer. She was talking to Nirmala about how to repel raccoons. She didn't want her frogs turned into dinner.

Nirmala was standing at the fence, looking at the little fountain shaped like a rocky waterfall with ledges, as water cascaded into the pond.

"Bukajeet's uncle called. He wants me to take Bukajeet back. I wondered how long Uncle would put up with him. I told him to find someone else because he isn't coming here." Nirmala was so relieved that Bukajeet wasn't her problem anymore. Nothing could make her change her mind. While he was away in his own mad, alcoholic world, she was in a garden, contemplating a tranquil water fountain.

Nirmala smiled at her friend. "Your pond looks pretty. It sounds nice too."

"We'll bring the girls out here when they get home." Susan was helping with the children now that Nirmala was on her own.

"It shouldn't be so hard to keep children safe at school," said Nirmala. "It wasn't like this when I was a girl."

Susan thought about her high school in the suburbs of Toronto, way out in Scarberia. She remembered as a girl riding a horse through pastoral meadows, across creeks at Kennedy and Steeles. Nothing left of that.

"You know, Nirmala, at this point, legalizing pot is the only way to take control. He who controls the cash flow has the power."

Nirmala frowned and said, "It isn't right for drugs to be legal. They should be illegal. How could they be legal? That would be saying it's alright to do drugs. We don't want that."

"The trouble is," said Susan, "the laws that make it illegal don't work the way we want them to. They can't keep the drug business out of high schools, for one thing. The other thing is: Why can't they be legal? What's wrong with saying that these drugs exist in our economy? We want to control their production, distribution, and use. Why should psychopaths get all the money? What's this morality that we think we're upholding by making people criminals? Truly, there has to be another way."

This was on the afternoon of the shooting.

That night, Susan woke briefly to see Mark putting on his pants and shirt. "Ralph needs to go out. I shouldn't have given him that steak. He's getting so old. I'll just be a minute, sweetie. You go back to sleep." She had nodded off for what felt like a second before the sound of explosions filled the night. She bolted out of bed to plaster her face to the window. Susan looked out only long enough to realize that she couldn't see anything, but she heard a car tearing away. She didn't even get her housecoat, just ran outside in her pajamas.

Her heart stopped when she saw Ralph lying over Mark's chest, covering the wound like a blanket. She realized that Ralph had been shot as well, trying to save her beloved husband. For one brief moment, she was happy that Mark and Ralph had passed on together. Then her heart broke. The overwhelming loss hit her. She didn't remember much after that.

Only Nirmala and Susan went to Gurlochan's funeral. He had been found shot in the head underneath the Queensborough Bridge. He was assassinated four days after Mark was gunned down; the killer had mistaken Mark for him. No one except Nirmala had truly grieved for Gurlochan. She grieved for what he should or could have been if the promise of a Canadian education didn't include tiptoeing through the minefields of an illegal multi-level drug-dispensing business. Susan was too numb to care about anything, but certainly, seeking vengeance for her loss was not on her mind. What vengeance could restore anything to her, to Mark, to Nirmala, to Gurlochan, to anyone? All was lost.

The infamous Los Diablos gang went on to greater criminality. They dropped the name and changed their look to sophisticated metro man with stylish goatees and artistic sideburns. By the time they got into their twenties, they were the invincible young swags of Main Street. They owned their share of paradise, manoeuvring gleefully in their hot rod cars, blaring *bhangra*, wearing natty clothes, all primped and preened. They flashed about like little gods of the golden land.

The wheels of justice do seem to grind slowly, thought Susan, but finally, Razinder and his boys ended up charged with crimes. For a brief while, it seemed that justice would prevail. Then came the Gillian Guess Show. The Los Diablos boys all got off.

The Gillian Guess "Show" was a tawdry love affair between a married man with a family, on trial for serious crimes, who winked at a bored, lonely matron of West Vancouver, who was on the jury. Everyone in Vancouver, and the world, watched this ridiculous romance turn a court of justice into a high school cafeteria. Conduct unbecoming notwithstanding, Gillian Guess did not understand that these men were on trial for more than what they were charged with. Everyone living in South Hill would have found them guilty.

Gillian Guess went on to do the Oprah show or was it some cable show? No one cared after the scandal died away.

Getting away with murder didn't deter the drug dealers of Main and 49th. Back to business, they fired their guns at a Hell's Angels club house, a western divisional headquarters. They also kidnapped the sister of the head of one of the most powerful drug-gang triads on the west coast of North America, if not the world; these boys having ties to Hong Kong and beyond. Doubt and controversy still exist over who killed off the Los Diablos. One by one, they were gunned down in front of their homes; in night clubs in front of hundreds of innocent people; at weddings in local halls, injuring children and ruining the happy day; and at night, driving down the city's streets. They are all dead.

Susan and Nirmala were raking the front yards. Susan stopped to look at the fallen leaves, still wondrous after life ebbs away from their veins, their skin, their form, changing from dazzling golds, reds, and oranges to brown ashes, to be absorbed back into the earth.

"We've both lost everything we ever hoped for in ways we never could have imagined back when we were young. Well, I'm glad we still have each other." Susan reached for Nirmala's outstretched hand. They clasped hands, warmly smiling at each other.

"We have the girls to live for," said Nirmala. "They will marry for love or they will not marry, if that's what they choose. They will be free to make their own choices."

The Dogs of Main Street

There is an adult-only, dog-friendly condo complex near Main Street called Kew Gardens, which has this amazing hot tub, set in a gorgeous, landscaped courtyard. All of the surrounding apartments have bay windows framed by wooden shutters done in a tasteful purple-brown. The exterior walls are a muted grayish-teal. The building blends into the verdant garden, a lush, vibrant, growing profusion with dashes of dazzling colour scattered throughout. At the far western end of this crafted jungle, under an octagonal glass and wood-beam roof, sits the hot tub, steaming and bubbling like a hot spring: a delightfully inviting beacon of the good life.

Prospective condo buyers all dream the same dream — they see themselves lying in this hot tub after a hard day's work, the mist rising from the soothing water, the gorgeous garden splayed before them, maybe add a couple of frosties. . . Oh, the joy. But these poor innocents aren't aware of one thing, and that is Mrs. Pinkel. Though in a condo at the other end of the complex, she is still close enough to lodge complaints to the strata council whenever anyone actually uses it. Her complaints have included too many people making sounds, leaving a mess and overstaying the 9 p.m. closure rule. Not 11 p.m. anymore. She'd had to campaign ruthlessly for that rule amendment. It had almost worn her out, she was happy to tell anyone who'd listen. Worn her right out getting that rule fixed, and what was the point of a rule if it wasn't enforced.

That was but one of many rules that Mrs. Pinkel was personally responsible for during her twenty-year tenure on the strata council. Rules were meant for a reason, she used to say, until a certain person had laughed and said, "Some rules are more honoured in the breach."

That laughter had spoiled it for her. That person, to her chagrin, lived in an apartment on the opposite side from her. That Laurie Freeman and her dog Sam.

Laurie loved her dog. He had long, droopy ears that reached the floor, a long body, a big head with a great big snout, and no legs, just feet and a tail. His legs got bred away, his ancestors having been fashioned to have no legs so that they could run through tunnels. Now, there are no tunnels but they still have no legs. Sam was Laurie's best friend. He came to live with her when he was just a tiny puppy. He only knew her. He loved her. And she loved him back. Sam and Laurie. For life. Sam was not just another commodity to Laurie. He was an animal deserving of respect, who depended on her. There was no price tag attached to Sam, in her mind. No way of breaking the bond, the trust, the affection, the friendship. Sam, though a dog, was a fellow traveller on her road of life, on this our Mother Earth, who provides all living creatures with what they need to survive. Sam needed her.

Laurie woke each morning at 6 a.m. and began preparations for her daily criminal activity: make coffee, put it in a carry cup, don long underwear, fleece pants, rain pants, long-sleeved thermal T-shirt, hoody, fleece and rain jacket., Then she'd get her winter hat with the ear flaps, before putting on cotton socks, with woollen socks over top, to stuff her swaddled feet into waterproof hiking boots. Then she'd gather the accoutrements of crime — a dog leash, poop bag, watch, flashlight, house key, cell phone, ball and ball chucker. And she'd be all set to go. Meanwhile, her partner in crime would be sitting patiently at the door, staring at it intently, then watching her intently, then at the door intently, then watching her. Good old Sam. No more eager, enthusiastic accomplice could possibly be found.

On this particular Sunday morning, Laurie opened the door of her condo and Sam ambled out, just as Mrs. Pinkel came down the hall. Laurie's first thought was, "What on earth is she doing over here?" which was followed quickly by, "Busted." Caught out at 6:30 a.m. on a Sunday by the harridan of Kew Gardens.

"Sam, sit." Sam sat in the middle of the hallway. Laurie fastened his leash.

"Well," said Mrs. Pinkel. "You know what this means."

"Yeah, it means I'm going to have to waste time talking to you," thought Laurie, but said, oiling the wheels of civil discourse, "Good morning, Mrs. Pinkel." She looked down at Sam, sitting patiently. His tail brushed the floor as it wagged back and forth in hopeful anticipation. Mrs. Pinkel looked down briefly but saw nothing to interest her. Her focus was on the bad dog owner, not the dog.

"You're in trouble. That's what this means," continued Mrs. Pinkel, a malicious gleam in her beady eyes, her thin lips twitching to suppress her pleasure. "That dog was off its leash in the hall. You, of all people, should know better. It's against the rules, as well you know." She drew in a breath through her nose, a loud, prolonged sniff to punctuate her point and convey that her long-suffering tolerance had been sorely tested to its limit.

It wasn't that Mrs. Pinkel hated dogs particularly. It was just that she so loved her rules. For Mrs. Pinkel, rules epitomized cultured living. And so, she dutifully belonged to the strata council, attended all meetings faithfully, took meticulous notes to supplement her prodigious memory of every discussion that had ever taken place, and supported every bylaw created to aid in the regulation of every aspect of communal living. From hot tub to indoor parking, she had an opinion concerning the proper conduct of her neighbours. Not just an opinion, she argued. Her contribution was based on well-informed, well-intentioned, impartial reason, and thus, a contribution over and above mere opinion. There was no noise too slight, no weed too small, no dirt too negligible that it escaped her well-considered, well-informed reason for a rule. It usually wasn't personal. She was impartial in her censure, inclusive in her criticism, and democratic in her tyranny.

"I'm going to have to write you up," she said, her delight barely contained. Her face was set in prim confidence, mouth slightly puckered and pulled downwards, head tilted to gaze righteously down her long, patrician nose. Her dignified bearing was diminished by her large ears, with their absurdly long, drooping earlobes dangling above her shoulders from a lifetime of wearing heavy earrings. But Mrs. Pinkel wasn't looking in a mirror, she was looking at Laurie Freeman.

"Of course you are," replied Laurie. She looked down at poor Sam, sitting with infinite patience, waiting for his walk, and he looked back at her, his soulful eyes full of compassion for her plight. They both looked over at Mrs. Pinkel, looked back at each other, and sighed in perfect agreement.

"Do what you have to do, Mrs Pinkel." Laurie's eyes looked over and beyond Mrs. Pinkel's shoulders, down the hallway to the beckoning exit.

Mrs. Pinkel looked at her with palpable loathing, her eyebrows pressing together leaving a deep crevasse between her hardened eyes. "You seem to think the rules don't apply to you."

Laurie had learned the hard way that unless you are a miserable masochist with no other option for annoying, exasperating pain, limit your proximity to Mrs. Pinkel. Everyone avoided her like the plague of locusts that she was.

"C'mon Sam, let's go." Sam rose up onto his four feet, his head, with its long snout, perked up with happy anticipation of balls to chase and bushes to sniff.

Laurie left Mrs. Pinkel standing in the hallway, staring at her back as she and Sam headed to the door. Mrs. Pinkel's hatred glared through her squinty eyes. Oh, that Laurie Freeman. Mrs. Pinkel didn't really care about the dog; after all, it obediently listened to commands to sit, stand, come, and stop. It was that woman's carefree, breezy attitude, her live-and-let-live, mind-your-own-business, impersonal friendliness that got to Mrs. Pinkel. And her hair, all wild and unkempt. Didn't she ever go to a hairdresser? She didn't seem to be afraid of anything, least of all what her neighbours thought of her, and that just wasn't right. People were meant to be God-fearing or else they ended up as servants of the Devil.

Mrs. Pinkel resumed her morning patrol of Kew Gardens but Laurie Freeman, as usual, had ruined her enjoyment. She returned to her apartment to sit primly on her favourite chair, facing the window that looked out over Pelletier Park. She began her vigil waiting for the dog people to come with their chuckers and balls so that she could watch them playing, while seething with rage. Well, she'd had it. From now on, she'd be phoning the dog pound, city councillors, and anyone else she could find, demanding action to end, once and for all, the use of Pelletier Park by off-leash dogs and their irreverent owners, who were so high and mighty that they thought that rules could be broken without retribution. Well, they were about to find out what righteous rules were capable of. She'd see to that.

Laurie set off at a brisk pace. Fog hung in the air, stilling the trees, their leaves almost frozen, with no wind rustling. Just the calm quiet of a wet winter morning remained, the sun not yet risen; only grey lit up the clouds hanging heavily on the horizon. She walked eastwards towards Mountain View Cemetery, her mind mulling over the scene with Mrs. Pinkel-Finkel, that horrible woman, that rule-ridden demigod of other people's lives and business, living like a spider waiting to ensnare unsuspecting victims in her ubiquitous webs hanging throughout the condo complex. A Nasty Neighbour. Just ask anyone from a fascist state what it's like to have neighbours report you for wrong thinking, never mind the wrong colour socks.

Laurie set Sam free. As she walked along behind him, she indulged herself with rants all of the way to Mountain View, expanding her platform to the cemetery's recently enacted on-leash-at-all-times rule. She was defending not only her freedom, but Sam's as well. Not to mention the rights of other mammals. If people can't live with dogs, what hope is there for bears, whales, elephants and tigers. Off-leash, on-leash. Off-leash, on-leash. The debate rages while the world burns. Not to mention how dog walkers patrol Mountain View, providing a community policing service. Everyone belongs to Block Watch. Dog people always stop to chit-chat about their dogs and all of the doings in the neighbourhood.

Sam ran ahead through the fog. Laurie could just make out the shape of another dog. It looked like Dex, the rescued Greyhound, racing towards them. She slowed to a saunter, peering into the mist to make out the shape of a person. Slowly, it materialized.

"Hi, Donna." Laurie recognized her rain gear. Donna and Dex took early morning walks in Mountain View too, and their paths crossed from time to time.

"Hi, Laurie. Hi, Sam."

As a criminal organization, off-leash dog walkers are an epitome of anarchy. They simply fulfill their heart's pleasure, in their own way, with no bureaucracy, no hierarchy, no dictates other than those that reflective of common sense and courtesy, united simply by their love of a companion animal.

"How's it going?" asked Laurie.

"Oh, pretty good. How about you?"

"Well I've been having a rant. I just got cited by Mrs. Pinkel for having Sam off-leash in the hallway."

"No kidding. How much is the fine?"

"A hundred. But I can get out of it. No one on the strata will cooperate with her."

"I had another run-in with that new guy they have working for the cemetery," said Donna. "I've just about had it with him."

"That short guy with the red hair and kind of red face?"

They both turned to head west, following the dogs to keep them in view.

"Yeah, that sounds like him," said Donna. Scorn in her voice. "First of all, he came speeding over in his car and just about ran me over. Then he jumped out and started yelling, 'This isn't a toilet for your dog to shit and piss in.' That's what he said. He comes up to me so his face is this far away from mine." She held up her hand a foot from her face.

"He's spitting into my face, 'You have no respect. No respect. This is a place people come to visit their loved ones. Your dog is shitting on their graves and pissing on the flowers.' I couldn't believe it."

They had stopped for Laurie to collect a big Sam poo into a black plastic doggie-doo bag. She tied the top flaps with a practiced motion. Then they were on their way again, walking towards the flagpole commemorating the Best and the Brightest, who lost their young lives for freedom, leaving the worst and dullest to carry on. They looped around it and headed east.

"So, I try to tell him that I always clean up and that I have respect. He just starts shouting louder at me, so I got defensive and started telling him about my Aunt Mabel."

Laurie deposited the black bag in a garbage bin, still listening to Donna.

"She's buried on the other side of 33rd and she loved dogs, absolutely loved dogs. He went berserk. Honestly. I thought he was going to hit me."

Donna had more to say as they walked down to the Brewery Creek dip, then up to the top of South Hill at 33rd and Fraser, pausing to take in the resplendent panorama, one of the most beautiful views in all of Vancouver. Rising out of the Burrard Inlet of the Salish Sea, they beheld the North Shore mountains. Dark full clouds were rolling in with the tide, blanketing the far westerly peaks. The two women turned away from the view, heading south down the path next to Fraser Street.

"I don't come here during the day when people are about," said Donna. "I come at the crack of dawn and never see anyone but other dog walkers. Really, if anyone's disrespectful, it's the guys jogging through here during the day. And what about lawn mowers? How respectful are they anyway?"

"What about the grave that someone dumps cigarette butts on?" asked Laurie. "I've seen it, over by Fraser and 33rd, right by Baby Carodoc." Laurie tossed a pinecone that had fallen from the giant trees lining the road. Sam went chasing after it with determination.

"The reason we're out here, and I'm not at home, cuddled up on the couch with a cup of coffee and the curtains closed, is because I'm a responsible dog owner. It's the ones that never take their dogs for a walk that are the real problem, not me or you. It's just so stupid." Donna gave an exasperated grunt, then said, "whatever" with a dismissive wave of her hands.

They left Mountain View, walking along 37th, past the little resting area on the bike route with a bench and some gardens planted with evergreen shrubs. They came to Soladog Lane, where they parted company with cheery good-byes and wagging tails.

On the way home, Laurie and Sam stopped at Pelletier Park. Sam was obsessed with chasing the ball, so Laurie threw it and Sam chased it. She was a slave to a dog who lived to chase balls. As they played, it began to rain.

Laurie couldn't see Mrs. Pinkel sitting in her chair, staring out the window, nor did she know that Mrs. Pinkel had tried to report her to the City but had been thwarted because it was Sunday morning. Laurie finished throwing the ball, continuing on her way, oblivious to Mrs. Pinkel watching her.

The rain fell harder and colder as Laurie finished Sam's morning walk. She didn't begrudge Sam his walks. After all, since she'd gotten Sam, she'd lost thirty pounds. Her blood pressure had returned to normal, as had her cholesterol. She'd stopped getting migraines, hot flashes, and back pain, and the insomnia had gone away. She walked seven kilometres a day, three hundred and fifty-two days a year. She calculated that she'd walked to Toronto and back, twice. She knew that her renewed good health was Sam's gift to her. It wasn't always easy to get up off the couch, especially on a cold, rainy winter night, but Laurie knew that once she got out, she would invariably start to enjoy herself. Somehow, even monsoon rain became a delight.

So, on Sunday evening at 8 p.m., as she looked out the window at the thick wall of water, Laurie had to dig deep for the will to go outside, but as always, she got herself ready for Sam's bedtime walk. No, she didn't begrudge Sam his walk, even on a cold, wet winter night with freezing water pounding down from thick dark clouds hanging in the trees.

Donning her rainproof dog-walking ensemble, Laurie turned on her flashlight before making her way out of the door. They walked with heads down towards Main Street, the rainwater running in streams and carrying leaves down the road. In some places, huge pools had formed. It was a deluge. Since she was bundled up in all of her gear, warm and dry inside, the weather didn't bother her. The outside was another matter. Even her umbrella had broken and she had thrown it in a garbage bin next to two other broken umbrellas.

And that's when Laurie's Sunday night routine began to take a sudden detour. She and Sam had just passed the driveway to the underground parking for the condo complex, where the building ended. A passageway sloped up between it and the next building and that's where Sam disappeared. Laurie didn't think too much at first. Sam had found something interesting to smell. She pulled her scarf up around her face to ward off the freezing rain.

Sam was gone for what seemed a long time. Laurie pulled her scarf down to call him. He didn't come right away. She called him again. The feeling that something wasn't right began to tingle in her stomach.

"Sam, come," she called with a hint of anxiety in her voice.

Sam appeared at the hedge that separated the lawn from the sidewalk.

"C'mon, let's go." Laurie was ready to make quick work of the rest of the walk.

But Sam wasn't having any of it. He disappeared again. It was too dark for her to see where he had gone. She shone her flashlight but it was too weak in the driving rain.

"Sam. Come. We're going." She used her no-nonsense alpha voice. But no Sam appeared.

"Sam, where are you?" Laurie began tromping into the black passageway, peering through the rain, swinging her flashlight back and forth. She went about ten metres.

"Sam?" She looked left and right, up and down. She couldn't see him. Then she heard a short, sharp woof behind her. She spun around. He was near the hedge.

"Oh, Sam. There you are. Whatever are you doing? Let's go home now. My Knowledge Network show is on soon. Come on, it's really cold." She walked back down the passageway but Sam stood his ground.

"What is it?" She was beginning to realize that she might be having a Lassie moment: Sam was trying to tell her something. She walked over to him, pointing the light under the hedge. Sam turned and began pawing at something on the ground. She came closer. It was almost covered with big chestnut leaves. She bent down and touched it. With growing horror, she realized that it was a body. The shock intensified as she saw that it was the body of Mrs. Pinkel. Sam began to lick the face of the old woman who groaned weakly but did not move.

"As it turned out," Laurie said to some dog people in Pelletier Park a few days later, "she was coming home from church and slipped and fell on some wet leaves on the sidewalk. She twisted her ankle. So she hopped up the passageway towards the nearest windows, trying to get someone to notice her. But she slipped on some more leaves and fell again. She rolled down the slope, landed under the hedge, and passed out. She had hypothermia when Sam found her. If he hadn't, she probably would have died."

Laurie looked at Sam, running across the park as fast as his little, stumpy legs would take him. "Yes, if Sam hadn't come along, she would have died."

"What was she doing out walking in that rainstorm?" asked Noel's dad, another slave to a ball-loving dog. He chucked a bright orange one for Noel, the black retriever, to chase.

"Well, I asked her the same question. She said she'd been walking home from church every Sunday for the last twenty years. You don't know her, but I doubt anyone offered to give her a lift. She's one of the nastiest people you'll ever meet. Really. I saw her neighbour from the apartment next door this morning. He told me that I should have left her there to die."

"What?" Noel's dad looked at her in disbelief.

"Oh, he was joking," she said. "Well, half-joking maybe. You have no idea what it's like to live in the same building as her. Believe me. But once Sam found her, I could hardly leave her there. I called an ambulance and went to the hospital with her and stayed while they got her settled for observation. I went back the next day and brought her home, made sure she got to bed, brought her some soup and bread, bought her some groceries. She has no one, not one person other than me to help her. Fortunately, she seems grateful. She hasn't said very much. In fact, she hardly talks at all but she looks happier. She's had a near-death experience."

Watching Sam bounding after the ball, they both laughed as he turned his long body around. Dogs are an endless source of fun and laughter, thought Laurie. Nothing is as joyful as a happy dog bounding after a ball, or a dog in snow, as some say.

Sitting in her chair by the window, a plaid blanket wrapped snugly around her knees, her feet encased in warm socks and woolly slippers, sat Mrs. Pinkel. She, too, was watching Sam with a joyful smile on her face.

Mountain View Madness

Michael Weinstein had done his run every morning for the last five years, never missing once because he never got sick. He now knew, with absolute certainty, that if he missed a day, he would get the flu and it would want to make up for all of the years that he had held it at bay with his lope around Vancouver's Mountain View Cemetery. He was fully aware of his superstition, using it as a playful tool to maintain a discipline that he enjoyed. The morning run was devotional worship. The joy he found in the movement of his body radiated into his life like so many beams of light and breaths of fresh air.

Michael's interest in his run had extended to Mountain View. He had joined the community group that formed to participate in the Master Plan for upgrades and beautification, and had watched the cemetery's children's brook unfold with satisfaction. He had investigated the Jewish cemetery enclosed by a hedge, as per tradition. He had tried to read the inscriptions on the brass plaques attached to the pillars of the Asian pagoda, before all of the brass was stolen. He knew the Masonic section, the 1918 Flu section, the shipwreck section, where infamous people were buried, and where the Musicians' Monument was located. He collected the stories of Mountain View like a boy stuffing his pockets with rocks and string. Of all the stories that piqued his interest, it was the grave at the top of the hill at Fraser and 33rd that he pondered relentlessly for years and years, the one next to Baby Carodoc.

Michael knew about Baby Carodoc, the first little soul to be buried in Mountain View, back before the turn of the century. As the story goes, the first person who should have been buried in Mountain View didn't make it up the hill from Fraser and 33rd. He was a big, overweight guy who'd died of alcoholism. His friends couldn't manage the coffin up through the bush so he was buried underneath the intersection, outside the gate.

It was the resting place next to Baby Carodoc that held Michael's interest. For years and years, someone had been dumping cigarette butts and beer bottles on it. He always ran by the big tree to see if he could catch the culprit in the act of desecrating the grave of Elio Benino, Beloved Husband and Father, Rest In Peace, defaced to read Rot In Hell.

Michael's pondering on the meaning of a pile of butts and brown bottles of Granville Island lager, left on a grave with a defaced gravestone, was professional in nature. He was a psychologist by trade, a fearless, tireless traveller into the foreign worlds in people's minds, an internationally acclaimed expert on delusion and the malfunction of the brain in all of its complexities. He had, along with his peers, spent his entire adult life exploring the dysfunction of family systems. He had participated in the identification of the pathologies that arise when children are raised by narcissistic, alcoholic parents. He was an expert in helping people find their way out of the miasma of lies, half-truths, and silence of emotional abuse, helping them accept that nothing but nothing is ever going to make their childhood anything but what it was. But this awareness didn't have to remain an unbearable pain; he let them know that some developmental damage can be repaired if people get support to change and grow. For people who hunker down into their rage and fear, life never gets better.

For Gordon Bryce, nothing ever went right. He woke each morning with a dull sense of dread that was quickly overlaid by a patina of annoyance. As the warmth of anger spread from his solar plexus to his feet, heart, and brain, he began to think about dog walkers and their animals pissing and shitting on graves, on people's loved ones buried beneath the ground, a big turd sitting on top. He felt completely justified to feel disgusted by the befouling of sacred ground by the shitting, pissing, defecating dogs and their stupid, stupid, ignorant owners. Oh, yes indeed, he, and only he, had the authority to apprehend, chastise, ticket, and fine these imbeciles as per regulations and his reckoning. He had a war to wage, battles to fight, tickets to write, and people to yell at. This familiar rant kept him going as he prepared for work and got into his car for the long commute to his job at Mountain View Cemetery in the centre of Vancouver. Today, for the first time since he could remember, he found that he had left ten minutes early.

Some people who live near Mountain View Cemetery are as punctual as Swiss clocks when it comes to their dog walking times. Joe Johnson, a husky and gregarious fire fighter, was one of them. Everything about the morning routine could vary except the time that he and his lovable mutt Jack left the house. Jack also had a route that he expected to take through Mountain View, through the hole in the hedge to the war memorial flagpole and the new war memorial monuments, then straight down the hill to where Brewery Creek flows beneath the ground in a culvert, then up the hill to Fraser, and out the gate at 33rd, before crossing the street to the north yard to return home. On this early, foggy and dark morning, for the first time ever, Joe and Jack were ten minutes late leaving.

It was a dark dawn of a grey day for everyone. Michael came running up the stairs at Fraser and 33rd and turned west to run along the cedar hedge bordering the fence, heading towards Baby Carodoc and Elio Benino. There, dumping a bag of cigarette butts, was a shadowy figure. Michael stood in his tracks. He couldn't believe his eyes. He blinked, astonished at his good fortune. The great mystery was solved. He walked forward, purposeful and intensely curious to see who wanted Elio, Beloved Husband and Father, to rot in hell under a pile of stinking cigarette butts.

"Hi," said Michael. The man didn't turn around. Michael moved around to face him. "I've been wondering who did this."

The swarthy man, in his fifties, scowled at Michael and said, "Now you know."

Michael's emotional feelers were wobbling. He stilled the front of his mind to let intuition rise up. Under the man's receding bloodshot eyes, drooped dark brown sacs of wrinkled skin. With black brows furrowed together, his eyes gleamed like smoldering coals ready to burn wildly. His mouth was turned down in a petulant pout. A drunk, a disintegrating alcoholic. Undoubtedly, he was once a fine figure of a man.

Now, he had a beer belly and flabby weak chin. He was holding a half-full beer bottle in one hand. Turning his back to Michael, he took a swig. Michael became acutely aware that he was wearing running gear, looking the picture of vitality and healthy living.

"Well," said Michael, as if rubbing his hands together. "That's your father."

In for a penny, in for a pound, thought Michael, suddenly remembering the English adage, a pound being equivalent to a dollar or loonie. He just had to know more. He decided to strike fast with clean, surgical precision. "You hated your father."

"He never gave a shit about me," said the guy. He kicked at the cigarette butts lying in a heap on Elio's grave. "Never cared what I thought or what I wanted. He always blamed me for everything. He blamed me for all his stupid mistakes and he made lots of them, believe you me. He was such an ignorant fool but he thought he knew everything. He always, always, had to be right, no matter what it was. Everything had to be about him. All roads led to Elio and then maybe Rome."

The man had said this to the gravestone, not to Michael. From the cadence and bitterness, contained like little bombs in certain words, Michael knew that this was a self-talk tape, looping around and around, caught in the brain like a sore that never heals, over and over again. *My father never gave a shit about me.* Narcissistic parents (mother in a fantasy bond, father with grandiose delusions) and children lost in a world of lies. Protecting the fantasy world is a horrible, mean man who will say anything and do anything to prove to his son that he is superior and always right. There can be no contradictions, nor criticisms. To back up these demands, father can hurt however and whenever he wants. Mother stares at the ceiling. Afterwards, she consoles her children by telling them not to upset him.

"All he ever did was criticize me," said the guy, still kicking butts. "'Why can't you do anything right?' he'd say all the time." Michael could hear the nasal tone moving up the scale as outrage reached hopelessness and remained in helplessness. A whining child for the duration of his life, his development halted by childhood trauma. His ship had sailed without him.

Joe Johnson came down the steps of the covered porch of his beautiful, four-storey, wooden house, built over a hundred years ago by a sea captain. At the top of the house was a little observatory with a telescope that the sea captain had looked out of, still there, after three owners. Joe had spent two years renovating the house and his wife loved him for it. He got to the sidewalk and turned to look with contentment at his happy home before striding forth towards Mountain View, following along behind Jack.

Gordon Bryce drove along 33rd, engaged in one of his driving habits, which was cursing at other drivers who he categorized into racist and sexist genres and themes related to lack of intelligence and courage. Like the moron rabbit in front of him who didn't know how to make a left-hand turn properly. Alert to the slightest danger, he drove in a state of hyper-vigilance, shouting aloud to people who could not hear his vile spew of hostility.

Michael was looking down at his running shoes and flimsy clothes. His shorts made him feel exposed and vulnerable. He looked up and around at the fog hanging thick in the gulley over Brewery Creek, at the big tree and all of the dark, eerie shadows in the dim gloaming with wisps of mists rising from the earth. Elio Benino's son finished the bottle of beer, turned suddenly, and threw it at the gravestone, where it shattered on the grave, on top of the pile of cigarette butts. He came lunging towards Michael, laughing as he'd pulled a fresh bottle from his pocket.

The hair on Michael's legs started to rise. His intuition suddenly reverberated with the realization that he was in a graveyard with a severely disturbed, violent drunk. Unlike at Colony Farm, where he worked with violent people who were criminally insane, he was, at this moment, bereft of support, the kind provided by locks and restraints.

"The jerk died before I had a chance to kill him." Wiping spittle from his mouth, the drunk advanced closer towards Michael.

"Then, as a final insult, the sadistic sick puke he was for his entire life, he cut me out of his will. Not one penny. I kid you not. It all went to my sister. She's just like him. I told her a thing or two. Until she apologizes, I'm not speaking to her. No way. She apologizes first."

"When did your mother die?" The nano-second the question fell out of his mouth, Michael knew that his neurotic need to know had quashed the red flag of fear. Never mind in-for-a penny, in-for-a-pound. It was more like, in for a Loonie, in for a Twoonie.

"My mother was a saint." More shouting at Elio's gravestone. "And he killed her. She loved me. We were happy when he was away. When he was around, all he did was yell and complain. She was his slave."

Michael knew this rant all too well. Textbook. Doting mother who allows her children to be hurt without defending them. Oh, the confusion, mixed messages, and crazed feelings.

Joe Johnson walked briskly past the flagpole to our boys who sacrificed their lives for the future of humanity, fighting against the forces of fascism. As a fire fighter, Joe understood putting life and limb on the line for his community, a responsibility he bore cheerfully. He loved his wife, his children, his dog, his house, his job, his neighbourhood, his city and his country, as well as the Montreal Canadiens. So what? He was from back east. What was he supposed to do, abandon his team just because he moved from Montreal to Vancouver? He'd gotten his start in life treeplanting and still headed out every summer in a camper truck to explore in the woods. He knew some beautiful spots in the mountains to take the family. The night before, they'd had their annual open house, always a big bash. Joe was savouring the memory as he walked towards Fraser and 33rd.

Gordon Bryce was a man of action. "Can do," he'd say. Off he'd go to do whatever he was told. He had been honoured with the duty of maintaining the sanctity of Mountain View from dog excrement. He headed towards the lights at Fraser and 33rd with missionary zeal, hoping to catch the green before it changed. Impatient with the idiot driver in front of him, he considered whether to zip past, then cut her off to teach her a lesson, but abandoned the idea when he saw that she had sped up in response to his tailgating.

Michael stood knobby-kneed in running shoes. The drunk threw another beer bottle, swearing and spitting, kicking at the cigarette butts. After decades of meditation, as a long-time practitioner of compassion and loving kindness, Michael now found himself folding his hands into fists and reclaiming his legs from fear. After all, he was an athlete and Butt-guy was a flabby drunk. His empathy energy was now focused like a laser beam on his own survival as his synapses assessed his forward line-up, his defensive backup and the goal —to leave as quickly as possible.

Joe Johnson followed behind Jack down the path towards Brewery Creek, down through the fog, where it rose up from the underground stream, thick and grey. Jack bounded ahead sniffing everything and peeing everywhere, while Joe was lost in a reverie of the delicious party food they had consumed the night before. There had been fourty-four guests; some were from work, some from his wife's work, some neighbours, but mostly friends from the last thirty-five years. A great group of people. And the food. Oh, the potluck food. The prime rib he had barbequed had been gone in what seemed like minutes. There had been t-bone steaks; stuffed pork chops; Maui ribs; platters of sushi; plates of every type of cheese imaginable; a tureen of clam chowder; shrimp cocktails; cocktails; a chocolate fondue with fresh local strawberries; wine; pies; breads; beer; and chips.

The sound of an angry, loud voice cut into Joe's memory of Black Forest cake with homemade vanilla ice cream. He lifted his head to see the top of the hill at 33rd. In the distance, just above the fog of Brewery Creek, he thought he could see two figures grappling in the shadows of the big tree. He wondered where Jack was. He whistled.

Gordon Bryce came careening in his car through the gate from 33rd into the fog patch, missing Joe, who he did not see. At the entrance to the cemetery, before the road dipped down, he thought he saw some figures under the big tree and possibly, a dog. He sped up the hill.

Butt-guy had decided he was going to leave too, as in, get in his car drunk as a skunk and drive off home, wherever that was. He'd performed his ritual. He'd told his father a thing or two and he expected an apology, if not in this world then most certainly in the next, where he would also have the opportunity to choke the life out of the miserable wretch. He swung around just as Michael began moving. They collided.

"See what you've done," shouted Butt-guy.

Michael covered his left eye with both hands, sure that he'd been blinded by the guy's watch, wrist, and hand smashing into the side of his face.

"What's the matter with you?" Butt-guy was struggling to keep his balance as he stumbled towards Michael, too stunned to move.

"Are you always that clumsy? Falling over yourself like that. Don't you know how to walk yet? Can't you do anything right?"

The drunk listed to the left, waving a beer bottle to the right. Michael, barely able to see, jumped out of his reach too slow, too late. The bottle landed on the side of his head, knocking him sideways.

"Now look what you've done."

Joe came out of the fog patch and watched the car ahead of him speed up the hill. He had seen two men staggering, one holding a beer bottle, and heard more yelling. He felt slightly bewildered at such drama so early in the morning. He whistled again for Jack, who, after sniffing at the men struggling by Elio Benino's grave and peeing at length on Elio's gravestone, lifted his head to the sound and obediently trotted off towards Joe.

Gordon Bryce couldn't believe his eyes. The dog was peeing on a gravestone. The moron idiot owner, instead of leashing his dog, allowed it to piss and shit on sacred ground. He was witness to this act of filth and degradation. He screeched to a stop, leapt out of his car, and ran pell-mell towards Michael and Butt-guy.

"How would you like someone to shit on your face?" he yelled at them.

Michael and the Butt-guy looked at the red-faced, red-haired, red-nosed man, shouting and running up the rise of the hill like a maniac.

"Oh, deny it," ranted Gordon. "Just try to deny it. Not with me. I saw it with my own eyes." His very own eyes. There was no denial possible in his world. None at all.

"Deny what?" said Butt-buy, belligerent and drawing his body up to its full height. Leaving was now forgotten.

Syncopation ran amok up Michael's spine. Pain receded into the background. The injuries were forgotten. He fled, on marathon feet, almost colliding with Joe, who'd breached the hill in record time and was seconds from disappearing through the little gate at 33rd and Fraser. Maniacal cries echoed in the misty fog. Joe had no intention of introducing Jack to the owner of those sounds.

"Oh, sorry, excuse me," said Michael. He kept going.

"No problem," said Joe. He kept going too.

"Your dog peed on the gravestone," said Gordon, settling his feet into the ground.

"I don't have a dog, you moron," said Butt-guy, still swaying but not stumbling anymore.

They were standing at Elio's grave.

"Listen, you idiot. I saw it. You can't deny it."

"Deny what? What is your problem?" He stretched out the words into a fight-picking challenge.

"*My* problem?" Gordon stepped forward, outrage pouring though his veins.

Drunk Butt-guy, still with bottle in hand, stood wobbling, waiting for him. After his blunder minutes before, he knew that this time, he had an effective weapon.

"Where's your respect?" asked Gordon. His spittle went flying as a gale force blew out the words. Deep down, he was thrilled that he now had permission to go hog-wild. He'd seen the crime with his own eyes.

Butt-guy gripped the bottle with all of the force and cunning of an abusive, damaged, crazed old drunk. With lots of muscle still hanging on his brittle bones, he looked at the little red-haired guy attacking him. He hated red hair. He popped Gordon on the side of the head and watched him crumple onto Elio Benino's grave, where he lay splayed on the cigarette butts and broken beer bottles. He spat on him.

"Just like my father." He kicked Gordon's right foot. Then he kicked the left foot a bit harder. He couldn't believe the satisfaction: he was kicking his father. He didn't have to follow him past the grave, after all, to give him what he deserved.

"Apologize," he said. He kicked again. "First, you apologize."

Gordon didn't answer.

"What's wrong with you?" he said. He rolled up some sticky, beery phlegm in his mouth. For the first time in his life, he felt happy.

Joe finished his walk, vowing never to be ten minutes late again. Maybe it was time for a new route, his wife said.

Michael went home and had a long, hot shower. He looked in the mirror at his black eye, felt the bump on his head, and laughed. In for a Loonie, in for a Twoonie – more fool you.

Main Street Mudras

It came to Sally when she was standing on her head that she and her yoga group should go on a retreat. "My family has a huge cabin out by Hope right up in the mountains. It's so beautiful."

Radha was busy helping Kathy with her first headstand. Kathy's shoulders had started out like earring-shoulders, hunched up so high they looked like they were dangling from her earlobes. Four years of yoga later, her shoulders had slowly lowered down and loosened up enough for a headstand, although her joy centres at the top of her lungs weren't opened up fully. They were working on that.

"Let's make it a yoga-party retreat," Sally said. She was lifting herself from a headstand into an effortless handstand.

"What a great idea. It'll be so much fun," said Kathy. She looked out from under her armpit, her head on the floor, her body in a pyramid, preparing to fling her legs up to be caught by Radha, who stood behind her, leaning against the wall.

Across the room, Terry was doing a headstand away from the wall, slowly twisting her body around from one side to the other, using her head as the anchor, with her legs together and raised towards the ceiling. She did the splits with her legs, then folded them into a full lotus, while still slowly twisting and arching her spine.

"I'll bring the vodka," she said. "I'll show you how to make a perfect martini. First, you put the vodka in." Terry and Kathy had discussed the perfect martini at length over a number of classes.

"No way," said Kathy. "I'm going up." Her legs kicked into the air. Radha caught them, then held her by her hips for stability while she balanced on the top of her head, stimulating the crown chakra. Kathy had only ever dreamed of doing headstands when she started taking yoga; back then, she was barely able to bend her body in any direction, though fit from riding her bike to work and innumerable gym workouts. "First you put the olive in. I've got a book." She was talking to Terry, her legs wobbling above her head, Radha holding them steady.

"So, what. What's a book? I went to a party and was given a martini-making lesson by the 2008 Best Bartender of Main Street." Terry lowered her legs from a headstand into an upside-down-L shape, then let her body relax into the pose, her feet, hips, and head in perfect balance.

"We'll have a martini-tasting contest. The panel of judges will let you know whose is best," said Sally. She was doing push-ups, from headstand to handstand, back down to headstand, then up again.

"Oh, great. A martooshi-mashing contest," said Terry.

Radha, still busy with Kathy, intoned in her mellifluous voice, "Focus on your breath, Sally. If you're not breathing, it's not yoga, though gymnastics is still fun too."

"My martishy is besher than yorsh," said Kathy. "I'm coming down." Her legs flailed to the floor.

"That was fantastic," said Radha, putting her hands on Kathy's shoulders to gently massage them. "That was wonderful." She always spoke sweetly from her warm heart, so it never mattered what she actually said, it always felt good. "You did your first headstand."

"That was amazing," said Kathy.

They all sang out a cheery note for Kathy's headstand, except for Nova.

"What about me?" she said peevishly. "I need some help from the teacher too." Then she smiled, but still looked unhappy.

They all looked at her and their collective shoulders sagged. What about you, they all thought, what about you, indeed. Nova was the low note of their Wednesday night yoga class. The class felt more like a private yoga club at Radha's little studio, just off Main Street, where they'd all been coming every week for years.

"Has everyone done their counterpose?" Radha asked. "We're going to move on to shoulder stand. We want to make this a meditation on tranquility. Norma, you said you weren't ready for headstand yet, have you changed your mind? Are you wanting help with a headstand now?" She moved over to where Norma lay.

"Nova," said Norma, lying with her legs up on the wall, resting.

"Oh, of course, of course, Nova." Nova had recently changed her name from Norma to Nova, coinciding with a surging interest in Kabalarian arithmetic.

"Nova," she was constantly reminding them, was a name with magic numbers that attracted love and light into her life. In spite of her reminders, she stayed Norma to all of them except Radha, who tried, but usually failed, to remember.

"Let's make some brownies as well," said Joanna quietly from the end of the room; she was already in a shoulder stand. "I have a recipe for brownies." She was moving her head from side to side while the rest of her body balanced above her, her legs together and raised high. Then she squiggled her shoulders together under her neck, slightly straightening her legs to deepen the asana.

"Doing yoga stoned can be extremely insightful," said Kathy. "That's how I realized my hamstrings are tight. When I was a teenager, my brother used to make fun of my legs."

"Really," said Terry. "Let's look at those legs. Well, no wonder your brother made fun of them."

Terry was doing her shoulder stand next to Kathy, who kicked Terry's foot. A playful skirmish ensued until their squabbling bodies fell over. Terry's legs flopped behind her head into a jellylike plough position while Kathy fell with a stiff thump against the wall. Their ongoing banter had never let up since the day they'd met. They often played like kittens, laughing and giggling, instead of holding the pose and staying with their breath.

"Close your eyes," Radha said in her soft, low and melodic yogini voice, moving away from Nova to lead the class in a meditation. "Extend the exhalation with a hum. Bring a vibration to your heart chakra. Imagine your body in balance. Balance between the material world of your body and the spiritual world of your energy."

"I'll bring the brownie mix and the beer," said Sally, who also played hockey on Friday nights.

"I'll bring the herb. I can get the best bud in town through a friend of a friend at work," said Kathy, who smoked one joint every Friday and only Friday night at eight o'clock. Then she fell asleep, watching late-night movies, completely forgetting about work, just dreaming about her full, rich life and all of the fun that she had planned for the weekend.

"I'll bring the olives," said Joanna, ever the foodie. They would be the most organic, most fairly traded, happiest olives ever procured from Main Street.

"OOO KKKK," Terry chanted, a blissful smile on her beatific face.

Nova said nothing, but her negative vibrations exuded from her tightly wrought body, dragged down by the weight of her ever-churning, disquieting thoughts.

They ended up on top of a mountain in a huge A-frame chalet, perched on a ledge on Paradise Mountain, overlooking the Similkameen River. They were standing in a circle on a magnificent cedar deck, watching the sun set behind the mountains, glowing red and orange.

"It's a great gift that we can feel beauty. Anyone at any time can look up and see the beauty of the clouds, the beauty of the blue sky," said Terry. She was smoking a joint.

"So true," said Kathy. "We can feel the beauty of creation. We can watch a sunset, our hearts touched by the beauty of Mother Earth. We actually feel beauty in our bodies. It's a truly awesome gift."

"It seems so obvious, but what would our lives be like if we couldn't?" said Joanna.

"It's a blessing and a gift that no matter how troubled we are, no matter how sad or discouraged we are, we can always look at the beauty of Mother Earth and feel uplifted," said Radha, taking the joint from Joanna.

"Well, I don't know about a gift per se," said Nova quickly, having firm views on spirituality, honed by ten years spent in a cult on Quadra Island; she had lived communally with a group of people who believed that they'd been specially picked by their omnipotent leader to be helper-stars bringing light to the world.

"Hey, look at the squirrel," said Terry. "He's got a nut in his mouth." She pointed to a nearby cedar tree. They all looked up.

"It's not a gift really," continued Nova. "You have to work for it. You have to do your spiritual work to receive that knowledge. Most people haven't evolved. They're sunk in a morass of greed and materialism. You think everyone can see what you see, but it's not true. You're special. You're a spiritual person."

Everyone looked at Radha, spiritual person, watching the squirrel with a joint at her lips. She paused her toke to say, "You don't have to be special to feel beauty. It's part of being human, it's part of our biological physiology. Anyone, any time, any place can feel the joy and wonder of Mother Earth."

"No, I don't think so. Most people couldn't care less about feeling beauty or appreciating a tree or whatever. They're just interested in living their consumer lives," said Nova.

"Well, that's their choice: to not experience. I'm saying the potential is a gift."

"Only if you've done your work. You're not honouring your spiritual growth."

"No. I guess I'm not."

"Well, you should."

"Should what?"

"Should honour your spiritual growth." She looked at Radha now trying to blow smoke rings.

"Should you be smoking that? Spiritual people don't smoke dope." She frowned unpleasantly. Radha smiled. "Well, there you go."

Radha looked over at Nova, not wanting to explain or justify herself. A little part of her, at this moment of the unfolding, timeless now, wanted to plug her ears and go "blah, blah, blah" to block out the beam of negative energy pouring forth from Negatron Not-So-Norma Nova, a weapon of mass depression.

Sally, with her perky sociability, suggested that they go inside to do some stoned-insight yoga. They all agreed that it was a good idea.

"We're going to begin with standing poses," Radha said. "To ground ourselves and connect with Earth energies. Close your eyes and feel your feet. Breathe into your belly and lower back. Release the breath downwards with an open throat."

Kathy, Sally, Joanna, Terry, and Nova were standing on their yoga mats spread throughout the huge room with the cathedral ceiling. One whole wall, facing west, was a bank of floor-to-ceiling windows looking out on the mountains and valley.

As they balanced their torsos over their hips, breathing into their bellies, Radha could see them glowing with the golden energy that moves in softened bodies.

"Any insights?" she asked.

"I'm hungry," said Terry.

"She wants to bring on the brownies," said Joanna.

"Let's do some back bends, then make martinis. I'll show you how it's done," Kathy said.

"I love back bends," said Sally, springing into a full-blown Wheel with the athletic grace of a childhood spent dancing. She looked beautiful with her back arched. She lifted one leg up straight so that it stood as a pinnacle, framed by the sunset glowing red and purple behind the black silhouettes of the snow-tipped mountain peaks. It was one of those gifts of beauty. To see her was to feel the power of the gift. She gracefully scissored her legs up into a perfect handstand, remained still for ten seconds, then came slowly back down to her feet to stand in Mountain pose, her hands in prayer position at her heart.

Kathy was on the floor, her hands facing backwards beside her ears, trying to summon the energy to hoist herself into a back bend. She closed her eyes.

"Find your breath. On the exhalation, lift up," said Radha.

They all watched as Kathy rose into her first unassisted back bend, lifted through her shoulders, released her neck, and sank down into her legs to release her sacrum. She filled her lungs, starting at the bottom of her rib cage, moving upwards to the lobe tips underneath the clavicles. She had persevered for years. Her body had responded by slowly unlocking and unwinding.

Kathy came down in a heap. They all fell upon her, excited by her achievement. She was so happy that she was almost crying. A back bend. A middle-aged scientist masters a back bend. Anything is possible. "Where's those olives?" Kathy looked in triumph towards the kitchen.

"What about me?" said Nova. "I'd like some help doing a back bend."

"I'm making martinis," said Kathy.

"Not without me," said Terry, giving her a tiny shove in the shoulders, a baby check in a loving, endless hockey game.

"I'm getting brownies ready," said Joanna.

"I'll help you," said Radha. She moved over to where Nova had her yoga mat.

"I need three people," said Nova.

"I'll help. That makes two. You'll be fine," said Sally.

Disgruntled, Nova did a half-hearted back bend as Friday-night yoga practice dissolved into the making of the perfect martini, while mixing up a pan of stoned brownies.

Radha was bemused as the evening unfolded. Never in all of her years had a yoga retreat been anything but a serious and quiet reflection on spiritual endeavour. Here was a loud, rambunctious, squabbling merriment of fun for all. Except, of course, for Nova. She was now sitting in front of the fire, staring pensively at the flames, ignoring everyone and everything.

"What's the difference between a man whining at your door and a dog whining at your door?" asked Terry. Joke-swapping time had commenced hours before. Terry was telling them her comeback to blonde jokes.

"The dog stops whining when you let him in."

Nova stood up abruptly from the couch.

"I'm going to bed," she said, looking at them with accusing eyes as they all snorted with laughter.

"I'm tired and need a good night's sleep. I hope this doesn't go on all weekend." That was the parting shot as she flounced out of the room. Terry wagged her finger and mimicked her face. Everyone laughed. It wasn't nice, but neither was Nova Norma.

They laughed and laughed the whole evening, telling stories, sharing lives, getting stoned, drunk, and happy. When they finally meandered to bed at who knows what time, Radha felt so uplifted. Her belly ached from laughter. As yoga retreats went, she was enjoying the route this one was taking.

The next morning, long after dawn had lit the mountaintops, they sat dutifully on their yoga mats, following ancient routines as best they could. Radha had attended many a silent morning meditation but never because people were hung over. Hangover yoga — since when? "Let's just do a few Sun Salutations," she said.

"Then go for a long walk in fresh air," said Sally.

There was some grunting and groaning while Radha led them through the Prayer to the Soul. "I open my heart to the Sun, I honour the Earth." Slowly, they moved through the sequence. Slowly, their bodies awoke to the movement, to the yin and the yang, the up and the down, the right and the left, the drunk and the sober. They finished up with some alternate nostril breathing before chanting the seed sounds of the chakras.

"You know," said Terry, when they'd opened their eyes, "I think it's a gift that our bodies can vibrate to sound. Really, it's a gift that when we can sing and chant, we create joy in our bodies. I mean, really, when you think about it, it's amazing. We can vibrate our bodies into bliss. Singing isn't just sound, it's feeling. I think it's a gift."

"It is, isn't it?" said Kathy. "I've never really thought about it, but what would life be like if no one could sing?"

"Let's chant the Guyatri mantra," Radha said. "It brings light into our bodies." So they chanted a Tibetan mantra passed down for thousands of years from one monk to another in remote monasteries on top of frozen mountains, far away from the vagaries of civilization, safely hidden away. Until now, with the sacking of Tibet by the Han Chinese, the Guyatri mantra has been set loose into the world: Meditate on Light.

"You have to be one of the chosen to bring down the light," said Nova, after they'd finished and were sitting like little glowing buddhas.

"Anyone can chant mantras," Radha said.

"No, not really. Very few people would even consider chanting a mantra."

"It's still a choice."

"Because you've been chosen."

"Because *you've* chosen."

Quibbling semantics. It's not about thinking, Radha mused to herself. It's about being thought.

"Let's go for a walk," said Sally, jumping up to get on with the day.

They began a hike through the temperate rainforest of huge, ancient, towering trees, dripping moss from their branches, their trunks completely covered in living green. They went along a trail tracked out in cedar chips, the air fragrant with tree bark and wet, growing smells. They took in the cool, fresh air, breathing out mist, as they made their way under the canopy of a profusion of branches high above, embracing the calm resilience of life growing rich and full from the earth.

Along the way, Nova attached herself to Radha.

"You know, I came here for a yoga retreat, not a drunk feast. I'm disappointed in you. I thought you knew better."

Knew better. Radha knew that it is all about love and compassion, about moving energy and moving beyond, but what she really wanted to know was an elusive mystery to her. She was at a loss for words. She simply stared at Nova. There was an uncomfortable silence before something to say popped into her head.

"I only know that I don't know. I live with uncertainty, with knowing I can never know. I wish I knew better too."

Nova wasn't ready for glib deflections. "You're degrading yourself by doing drugs," she said. She fixed her face into a look of stolid concern and lowered her voice to tones of confidentiality. "I'm very worried about you."

"You know," said Radha, ignoring Nova's attempt at an intervention, "People say you need to find a teacher to guide you on your path to enlightenment, but really we need to be our own teachers. Be your own guru. Everything you need to know is revealed to you when you do your own yoga practice. You see, Norma, I mean, Nova, you come to a yoga class once a week, but you don't actually practice yoga, so that's why you feel the need to have a teacher."

Radha was warming to her topic. "People think that to be spiritual, you need to live in a cave to immerse yourself in contemplation. But we're women. We can't extricate ourselves from our families and our responsibilities to go away to become enlightened. We have to do it in the midst of the stress of our lives. We need to be mystic housewives, shamanic secretaries, celestial lawyers."

Radha was feeling considerable elation at this point, like she'd scored cosmic points in a universal debate. But it was short-lived, like all of transitory life.

Nova started to cry.

"Don't mind me," she said. "I've been doing work around abandonment. That's why I thought yoga would help. I carry it in my shoulders. It isn't easy for me, you know." She stopped and looked meaningfully at Radha, watching her closely from narrowed eyes.

"You're doing really well with your back bend," said Radha.

Terry shouted from up ahead, "A moose, a moose. I think I see a moose."

"C'mon. Let's go see the moose," said Radha, striding purposefully up the path. After twenty metres, she turned to see Nova still standing, glaring like a rabid fox. "Let's catch up," she called, but Nova just flounced around, heading the other way. Radha wondered if flowers turned their heads away when Norma passed by. She took a long, deep breath and exhaled slowly, pushing unpleasant thoughts out of her mind. There are lots of worthy applications for yoga-mind training, she thought.

Sally led everyone up the trail to a small meadow at the top of the ridge. They gathered on a little boulder to behold the northwest Pacific mountains surrounding them. The sky was growing gray with clouds gathering in the distance; a snow front was on the way. Behind them, the clouds were slowing eating away patches of blue sky. Soon, it would start snowing. Standing and watching the world before them, Terry accidentally slipped backwards off the rock, pulling Kathy with her. Because their inner puppies were only thinly below the surface, a scuffle ensued that eventually ended with everyone sitting on the ground in a circle, looking at a little, dead dried-brown Lomatium plant. It was already hibernating until next spring, its pert head of seeds still standing upright. When a rare plant with medicinal powers shows itself, it's always cause for celebration. They sat meditating on the potent gifts that all life on Mother Earth shares, having evolved together in a web of relationships.

Snowflakes started fluttering on the hike back down the mountain to the cabin. Magical snowflakes filled the air, landing on their heads and tongues, their cheeks rosy, their lips red, eyes bright and faces shining with happy laughter. Down the twisty path they went, over boulders and rocks, then back into the forest over tree roots and tree stumps, down the path between the giant trees with their huge arms collecting the snow, sheltering them. They made their way as the light turned into a dusky grey with misty vapour patches. The path ahead became invisible but they just walked along, knowing that it would take them home.

They spilled into the cabin like a bunch of roly-poly bear cubs, all looking forward to their creature comforts. There to meet them was a grumpy frog, scrunched up on a chair, ready to flick out its tongue to snap flies.

"When are we going to do yoga?" asked Nova. "I hope you have something planned. This is supposed to be a yoga retreat and I'm expecting yoga. Unless that's too much to expect."

She squinted at Radha, speaking through compressed lips, "Is this a real yoga retreat?"

Radha sighed, at a loss for words. She was saved by Terry, who skated into the room, waving a fattie.

"I've got a doobie-doobie-doo," she said. She did a happy dance.

Dour, sour Nova swung her face towards Terry and hissed, "Are you a drug addict?" Terry burst into laughter. "Why? You got some crack cocaine stuffed up your bum?"

Faces twitched as they all tried to clamp their lips together, to no avail. The guffaws squeaked out the corners of their mouths.

"You people make me sick. Look at you, using drugs and alcohol on a yoga retreat. What kind of hypocrites are you? You know nothing about spirituality or spiritual growth or spiritual anything. I'm just wasting my time here. I want nothing to do with this. . .this . . . ." She paused as she groped for fitting words. ". . .This depraved debauchery." Nova delivered this insult with all of the force of her conviction, condemning them as demons of the hell realms.

"And you." She pointed at Radha. "I'm very disappointed in you."

Nova, a schoolteacher, had more than once stood with her arm outstretched, making judgments of impending doom with all of the petty tyranny that bad teachers can summon to their will and direct towards a hapless child.

"Oh, for Pete's sake, lighten up. Who cares about spirituality right now? Let's just have fun," said Terry.

"I cannot stay here another minute," spat Nova. "Not one more minute." She paused. Nothing. More silence. More nothing. They knew that she was expecting to hear an apology, but all she got was a pointed silence.

"Fine." Nova stomped off to her bedroom to pack her things.

The rest of the group was having a cup of tea together by the time she came out with her stuff. There was a collective sigh and a shrug of resignation.

"Don't go, Nova. We want you to stay. We can work something out," said Radha. "It's snowing out. It's night. We're on a mountain. It's not a wise thing to do."

"Why don't you take my mother's suite at the top of the cabin?" said Sally. "It has a king-size bed, a jacuzzi jet bath, and a television with satellite reception. You can watch movies, or there's books and magazines. There's lots of good food. You can still have a nice evening, even if you don't want to talk to us or hang out with us. Please stay. It's dangerous to leave now."

Nova would have none of it. She put on a determined face. Warding off their pleas, she loaded up Teresa, her little Toyota Tercel, turned it around, and headed down the driveway towards the road. She skidded a bit, but it wasn't a big deal. She was in complete control.

They started the evening yoga while the snow fell outside, dancing and dazzling in the huge windows. Flames, a half-metre high in the fireplace, glowed in reflections in the glass. The women settled on their feet, content to do some standing poses, moving into Half moon poses to send energy spiralling through their supple bodies. The compelling, resonant voice of Boris, the Russian Rocker, sang "O mani padme om," as they rotated their hips and opened their energy centres. After Boris, Terry put on Gabrielle Roth, lit candles all over the room, and cleared away as much furniture as she could. "Let's dance," she said.

Nova was inching down the steep road, barely able to keep the car from sliding into the ditch. She was completely focused, her hands gripping the steering wheel, her neck hyper-extended, craning forward as if it would make her see better in the blinding, swirling snow. She wished that she had gassed up. All she needed was to run out of gas and she'd freeze to death. A little bit of fear was beginning to replace her rage.

Up on the mountain, they were dancing their bodies into trances. Drum beats filled the cabin with speakers on every corner booming out the tribal rhythm. Their bodies flowed into serious grooves that led them upward and outward as they went deeper into the physical movement, their energies soaring into realms of joyous ecstasy.

"Ok, I'm scared now," Nova said to herself. She did an internal poke about for anger and found none. Uneasiness was growing, but no full-scale anxiety. Anyone would feel concern trying to drive down a mountainside at night in a white-out with no snow tires on their little Teresa Tercel, who was doing her best to keep moving forward. But Norma thought that the heater was not heating things the way it used to. She was definitely starting to feel more anxiety than uneasiness, but she could manage. She'd been through worse before. She'd be fine once she got to the highway.

They stripped off their clothes in front of the fire and headed to the hot tub on the deck outside. They laughed as they tiptoed barefoot through the snow, their feet tingling, goose bumps quickly forming, puckering up their skin. They stretched out their arms in defiance to the cold, embracing the snowflakes fluttering and flickering all around them. Then they sank into the deliciously hot, bubbling water, oohing and ahhing and sighing in delectable, sensual pleasure.

Nova leaned her head against the steering wheel as she gazed unseeingly at the freaking snow. A flat tire. Norma didn't use bad words, but the f-word was blowing on the cold wind that came in through the cracks in poor Teresa's old body. She cursed herself for not putting on those all-weather tires before coming, but that quickly digressed to how much she hated those women up on that mountain turning her yoga retreat into a sordid Surrey weekend of booze, drugs and fun before all else. What was wrong with them, what was wrong with her, what was she going to do? Her head was getting cold and sore from pressing on the steering wheel. She knew that she was going to have to get out of the car to walk into town. No one was going to be driving this road. Only her. The f-word sounded aloud and she wondered who had said it.

The women lounged in the hot tub for a couple of hours. Eventually, some martinis had made their way outside. Sally had opted for a beer. The martini thing was just a fad; she'd be sticking to the tried and true. Everyone had their little sips until the carbonated Whistler mineral water came out They greeted it with great joy, followed by homemade nachos and dip, then baguette and organic brie from the Comox Valley, smoked salmon from Gitxsan territory, and organic blueberries and ice cream from the Fraser Valley. They ate the entire feast while they dangled about the hot tub. Sometimes, they lay in the snow, letting the cold caress their heated skin, breathing deeply and exhaling, looking up at the snowflakes twinkling in the deck lights.

Nova's toes were frostbitten, she was certain. She had no feeling left in them, but her hands ached with cold and she had a wind-chill headache. After leaving her car on the side of the mountain, she had been walking in the snowstorm for what seemed like hours on end. The wind was so cold it had dried her sinuses in seconds. She had to keep her head swaddled in a scarf. Thank god she had her scarf, but she wished to god that she had better gloves. Her hands were frozen. She couldn't keep them warm. She plodded down the road, wishing that she had a flashlight, stumbling into posts and over shrubs and rocks, totally frightened. Nova's whole body had exploded into a full-on anxiety attack. She could hardly breathe. She thought that she was going to die and she hoped that someone would drive by.

They were in their pajamas in front of the fire, drinking hot chocolate, their bodies warm and contented. They cuddled in the soft pillows of the couches and easy chairs that they'd drawn up around the fireplace. Sally added logs to the fire while Terry put marshmallows in everyone's cup. They had found that quiet serenity that comes in the dark night when it's snowing outside, when the world is hushed as the snow piles up, covering everything in a clean, silent blanket of austere beauty.

Nova was trudging along in a nightmare world. She hated the forest, she hated the snow, she hated the cold, she hated yoga, she hated her job, she especially hated school children, she hated Main Street, she hated her stupid car, she hated her neighbours, and so what if she died. No one would care. No one. Nobody liked her. And she started to cry, but had to stop because the tears froze on her checks.

The group's mood was philosophical now as they chatted. Terry was sitting on the floor in front of the fire with Kathy lying next to her. Sally was stretched out on the couch. Joanna was curled in a papasan chair and Radha was reclining in a lazy-boy. They sipped their cocoa, telling most-embarrassing-moments-in-my-life stories, which naturally led to my-scar-is-bigger-than-yours tales, with body parts flashing in warm comfort and relaxed companionship.

Nova sat in the lobby of the police station in Hope, B.C., wrapped in a thin blanket that an officer had given her. She was sipping watery, lukewarm hot chocolate from a vending machine and trying not to cry, now that the ordeal was over. A tow truck driver going by had rescued her. He'd dropped her off at the police station instead of a hotel because she'd somehow left her wallet in the car. She could not face that it might have been lost in a snowdrift during her battle with the blizzard. She wanted to sleep but the chair was too uncomfortable and the lights too bright and an incessant, irritating noise was coming from the radio. Nova wished that she had someone she could call, someone who would come and take her away to a better world, who would put loving arms around her aching shoulders and massage the pain in her throbbing neck. She hated everyone who had what she didn't. It wasn't fair. A lump of envy formed in the pit of her stomach, then moved upward, hardening her heart. She hated herself and she hated her life.

"I think happiness is a gift," said Terry, wearing purple-penguin, flannel pajamas and fuzzy slippers, arching her back into the warmth of the flames from the crackling logs. "And friendship. If we didn't have both of these in the world, it would be a much different place."

"To good friends and good times," she said, raising her mug of cocoa, fortified with melted marshmallows. All of the women lifted their mugs and clinked them together.

Main Street Mining

Down on Main Street, by the bus station at Terminal, a couple of bars have been there forever. One is the good old American Hotel, an eternal landmark for just about everyone in Vancouver. Across the street is a neon sign, long broken, that flashes a dazzling G rls G rls G rls. Spelling isn't what matters on this block. Here, girls stagger on teetery high heels, dressed for success in short-shorts, their skeletal bodies exposed, their eyes unseeing.

The American Hotel is just a few blocks away from the infamous Main and Hastings international drug market. After all, Vancouver is a port. Ships come here from all over the world. Main and Hastings has the Vancouver Police Department building on one corner and Carnegie Community Centre on the other, balancing the forces of good and evil. The drug money passing through the neigbourhood makes it one of the wealthiest postal codes of unreported income in the world, on one hand; on the other, you will find some of the poorest people in Canada, making it the postal code of lowest-reported income. The truth requires knowledge of both sides of the coin.

People are always milling around in front of Carnegie. Anything and everything is for sale, leaving crack cocaine carnage and crystal meth death. Near the Georgia Viaduct is the Jimi Hendrix Museum. He lived there with his mother when he was a child. He stayed at home and played his guitar, but ended up a junkie anyway.

John Crawford was in the American Hotel, waiting for a shipment coming down from the north, which would arrive before midnight. He had to pick it up at the bus station and make sure it was on the plane with him the next morning. The American was a great place to while away some time. He was buying beer for himself and a guy he had met, sitting at a table at the back of the bar. The guy had a cheerful smile and a bouncy way about him. He was old but still could move around. He liked telling jokes, gossip, stories, even puns, just for a laugh. He liked to laugh, have a laugh, tell a laugh, and just plain laugh. Compared to the G rls, he was a much better bet for company.

The guy was an old-timer who had worked in the bush all of his life before recently retiring. He'd spent less than a year at a desk in an office in downtown Vancouver before packing it in. For the last few years, he spent part of his time at his place in Costa Rica and part in his condo in Coal Harbour. He was beginning to like Costa Rica more, but he couldn't let go of Vancouver.

John had got talking to him when he'd made a joke about the hockey game on TV later that night. Carl, though born long ago in eastern Europe, was a Canucks fan. John, born and raised in Edmonton, was an Oilers fan at heart, but since he'd moved to Vancouver, he was a Canucks fan now, though not wholeheartedly. He could still think ill of them in a way that he never would about the Oilers. However, since the glory Gretzky days, there wasn't much to cheer about. The Great One had moved to L.A. to marry an actress instead of living out his days in Edmonton. John couldn't blame him, but still, it changed things for the fans.

Now the Canucks had made it to the Stanley Cup playoffs. John was elated. It seemed miraculous. They had a good team, even if they usually caved in the last period. They could take a five-goal lead and turn it into a game lost in the last five minutes. They could not be relied on to make it to the finish. That was the sad truth. It was a jolt to watch. It was only natural for John to mention this to the guy sitting next to him. One thing led to another, and they discovered that they had both worked in mining exploration. Carl had retired from a life of exploring northern B.C. with a magnetometer, an instrument used to measure the direction or strength of a magnetic field. He'd done some international work too. He knew the area that John was headed to the next day: Dease Lake.

John took the beer back to the table and sat down. He and Carl both took some gulps and wiped their lips. Good beer. They were happy to have met. They'd already spent some time bemoaning desk work in the mining exploration offices over on Howe Street.

"Should be How-High Street," said Carl.

"Maybe Why Street," said John.

"Why-Bother Street."

"Or Who Street."

"Who and How Street."

John had just spent a month working the whole day, all twenty-four hours, expediting a project. He had only to pick up one last piece of equipment, a fragile meter reader, then he was heading for the Tanzilla plateau, the Grand Canyon of the Stikine, Mt. Edziza, Dease Lake, the Dease River, leading to the Liard River, and parts even further north and east in B.C. The Cassiar District has been attracting prospectors since the early 1800s. Carl was telling him about the 1970s, when consulting with the Tahltans was different than today. Back then, they just went where the provincial government told them they could go, which was everywhere. John could only imagine.

Carl and John had spent a couple of beers sharing tales of staking claims, racing helicopters, crazy trailblazing, and what-a-rush staking moments like hanging off a cliff to pound in a post or having it sucked down into the middle of a tundra bog. Carl told a couple of wild stories about the guys who had just come back from Viet Nam in the late 1970s. They took jobs as chopper pilots in northern B.C., flying like bats in dangerous ways that Canadian pilots didn't. They pushed the boundaries of the machine, flying in dense fog and into the rain. No visibility, no problem. So, stories of helicopter-crashes-they-had-known carried the two men into the early evening. The American was busy, the way it was every night, with lots of regulars, plus people passing through. The house band played good music. There was always some pool game being played. Everyone just wanted somewhere to drink and socialize.

Someone turned up the television. The Stanley Cup playoff game was starting. Carl and John looked around as Canada's national anthem lit up the air. Then the American anthem played. Everyone sung along to that too. The Canucks had made it to the Stanley Cup playoffs. Things were perking up. Carl and John sat up straight, moving their chairs to make sure that they had a good view.

"I'll tell you something about this business." Carl was talking about mining exploration, of course. He turned to look at John, who continued listening while he kept his eyes on the game. "This really happened. I kid you not. I only tell the truth."

Up on the TV, the players were taking their positions, getting ready for the puck to drop. Carl watched the face-off. It's a crucial moment. The stats say if a team scores in the first five minutes, they will win the game. The puck dropped and spun off into the Canucks' end. It was quickly fired down the ice. Both teams were skating fast, making sharp moves, pouring it on from the get-go.

"Back in the late seventies, I was in a camp up by King Mountain over towards Cry Lake, about a half-hour ride east of Dease. It was a big camp. Seven tents, maybe eight. The project manager was a guy named Pat Campbell. What a guy. He could talk you out of your boots. He could take the shirt off your back and then you'd ask him if he needed your skin too. A great guy to talk to.

"So there was him, two other geologists, two guys on loan doing an IP survey with two assistants, and two more kids, field assistants, who did soil sampling, plus the cook and me, doing a Mag ground survey." He was trying to count the number of people on his big sausage fingers. "What's that?"

"Ten," said John.

"Nine, if you don't count the pilot and the mechanic. It was a busy camp, everybody going off to work every day. Lots going on. Pat Campbell was the boss. It was his camp. He always knew what he was doing. He had experience, yesiree."

The referee called high sticking against Vancouver. John and Carl stopped the conversation to watch the power play. It was the middle of the first period. The whole place was more attentive now, watching the puck, waiting for a goal. This was the third game in the playoffs. Both teams had won one. John hoped he'd be watching the last game in the Tanzilla Pub in Dease Lake, not waiting to hear who won the Stanley Cup over a radio in the camp. They watched the puck get through the Canucks' goalie, who didn't even see it. He was looking the other way when it got sunk in from behind. 1-0. John wanted the Canucks to win but could easily see them losing. He didn't believe that they could truly make it to the end. They'd crumple, but hopefully, not before scoring some decent goals.

"It was the cook that found out first. These guys flew out from New York City for a big visitation. Three of them from head office were coming to check out the investment because it costs a lot to do what Pat Campbell was doing. We'd been there maybe two months by then. We had lots of work to do. Campbell kept us busy. He was one of those bosses. He went after the girls too, didn't matter what. So he was always after the cook. She was a university student just making some money in the summer to get through her education."

That was how John had got started too, doing summer work in the bush while he went to university, changing to geology and geophysics by his second year at UBC. Now he had a masters' degree.

Carl set his beer glass down.

"These three guys jump out of the Jet Ranger in these safari suits, like they're hunting tigers in Africa. For them, it's three, maybe four days of travelling. They're in the back of beyond. They can't believe they've finally made it all the way to the gold mining camp. Before they got out, it was just a dot on a map.

"Campbell told the cook to get coffee ready. They didn't come down to the cook shack so she loaded up a tray and took it up to Campbell's tent where the meeting was. That's how she overheard them talking about the Mag results being good, the IP survey showing anomalies, the soil samples supporting the rest of the results: all in all, a great investment so far.

"Well, the thing is, she came to our tent every night to play backgammon with Phil. They were doing a tournie to see who won the most games by the end of the season. So, I'd be graphing the Mag results. Jack, the geophysics guy would be plotting up the IP results. Sometimes she helped us. It's like doodling. She liked that kind of stuff. So she knew. The Mag survey showed squat. IP results had no anomalies whatsoever. The property was dead as a doornail.

"When those guys flew in, only the cook was in the camp. Everyone, me, Jack and his crew, the geologists, and all the assistants were long gone and well away into the bush working. She didn't usually do delivery but since they were the big mucketty-mucks, she thought she should up the service level. Otherwise, no one would ever have known. We would never have found out."

Carl leaned forward to talk to John in conspiratorial tones, resting his chin on his hands, elbows on the edge of the table. His story was coming out like he'd told it before, many times. John was leaning back in his chair, sipping his beer, watching the game while keeping the thread of the story, because dirty dealings were in the air. Something was going off the rails, over the handlebars, where one man's life becomes another man's story.

Loud, boisterous cheering rose up from everyone in the room after the Canucks scored. They watched the slo-mo instant replay of a pile-up in front of the net, the puck going into the crease while the defensive guys were incapacitated. It looked like someone's blade had tipped it in. People in the bar were animated. A large table of big guys next to Carl and John was having a blast. It was the end of the first period and the Canucks had evened it up 1-1. John started hoping that the Canucks might win. Could he dare believe that they could keep it together right to the end of the game and win?

"We were in our tent when she told us. Jack was playing his guitar. In the winter, he played in a band in Cape Breton, all kinds of occasions. He knew every song you could name. So, there was just me and Jack. We had to decide what to do. Can you imagine?

"All we decided was we wanted more information. We thought we could talk to the two geologists, Dan and Steve. They all worked for the same company. Me and Jack were sub-contracted. Not company men like they were.

"We went the next morning. Dan and Steve were getting soil samples ready to be shipped out. That was the kind of thing they did. They shipped out rock and soil samples, then went out looking for more. Jack was good at getting them to talk. They talked about all kinds of stuff. They seemed like nice guys. Just doing their work, like us.

"It took Jack a bit of time but he finally asked them if they thought anything was going on. They seemed shocked. Just like us. We all talked about what to do. They said they'd go talk to Campbell to see what he said. Me and Jack would wait in the cook shack for them. It seemed like a good idea at the time.

"We watched them go into Campbell's tent. We went down to the Cook Shack. We waited. We watched the three of them come out of Campbell's tent and head out of the camp north up the grid. We waited. We waited some more when who should appear alone? Campbell. He went straight into his tent. So me and Jack went up to ask him where Dan and Steve were. He told us he'd left them doing some work. We told him we'd heard from the cook about telling the head office a bunch of lies. Oh, he was some talker. Some charmer. We actually walked away believing his cockamamie hooey about marketing strategies and long-term planning. We went out to work thinking everything was copacetic. The only one left in camp was the cook. No one else was there when the chopper came. Flew in, picked Campbell up, and flew out again."

"He took off?" John was leaning forward now. Just how dirty had the dealings gotten?

"The cook saw Campbell take off, but not Dan and Steve. They weren't with him. He just jumped in the chopper when it came and took off.

"Steve and Dan didn't come back by dinner. That's when we began to get worried, wondering where they were. Jack went to radio for help. Campbell had ripped up the radio. We couldn't call out. No contact with the outside world."

There was another goal for the other side. It was the start of the second period. 2-1. The Canucks were losing. Some life went out of the room as the mood soured. It was more fun to win at pool than watch the Canucks lose the Stanley Cup. Complaining about the Canucks was more fun too. It was easy to yell at the TV. Get in there you guys. Play the game to win. Skate faster. Don't forget you're on a team. You make plays together. Carl and John listened to some of the grumblings from the crowd. No one wanted to lose.

John turned away from the TV. "What happened?"

"A guy from Northern Air came by right around sunset the next day. We used his radio to get help. We were four thousand feet up. It got cold at night and during the day sometimes. Back then, it snowed on July 1. We started looking for Dan and Steve. We had to keep looking for them until we heard that they'd been found. We looked for two weeks. We went out every day looking for them.

"Then we got the news. They flew us into Dease for a meeting. We were expecting the worst. We thought we were going to hear that Campbell had done something really wrong to them. Either that or they'd gotten very lost and been found too late.

"We crammed into the kitchen of the company trailer by the Dease air strip. There were two guys from the RCMP and all of us waiting to hear the news. No one was breathing. Everyone was still, listening. Well, instead of hearing about Dan and Steve getting lost in the bush, dying, unable to reach help, disappearing out there with the trees, the salal, the devil's club, the willows, the rocks, the creeks, we heard something we could hardly believe. They went to Mexico. They'd been on a sunny beach catching rays while we were slogging through the bush looking for them. We were out there in every kind of weather that you can imagine. Snow. Rain. Sleet. Blistering sun. You know what northern mountain weather is like. And they were lying on a tropical beach, drinking margaritas."

Carl laughed a big loud laugh. John had a laugh too. And life laughed as the Canucks scored a fantastic goal. 2-2. Everyone was wild and happy, cheering and hollering. Nothing like a good goal. The forward on a breakaway had deked left, then right, then made a clean shot to the top right of the net while the goalie was looking at the bottom left. Perfect goal. The replay showed its beauty. Stick-handling like a magician, skating full-on, two skates skimming the surface of the ice. He scores. It was the end of the second period. Dare to believe.

"What happened to Campbell?" John wanted to know. He was interested in the story now, which hinted of double-dipping, double-dealing, double-talking trouble.

"He got away. Jumped on a plane right out of the county. Someone said he was headed for tropical jungles to work for some dictator. He never came back here. He must have gone international."

"He probably ended up in Peru," said John.

"Or Paraguay."

"Chile."

"Columbia," said Carl. "He'd have fun there. Well, we had our fun too. After we heard the news, we got out the Johnny Walker. Jack got out his fiddle and had us doing the highland fling on the kitchen table. We never lost any money. It was paid work looking for them. You know how much they got away with?" This got John's attention away from the game. He turned to look at Carl for a moment.

"How much?"

"Two million, total."

Whew. Carl chortled and took a mouthful of beer, swallowing it with appreciation. He set his glass down on the table at the same time that John did. They both liked to pace themselves for long evenings.

"So who was in on it? How many shares? Start with the camp. How many in the camp were in on it?"

"Campbell, Dan, and Steve were in on the boondoggle. The helicopter pilot was only in on the exit strategy."

Everyone in the bar was ecstatic. The Canucks were winning 3-2. Third period. They'd scored another hockey-school classic with a forward set-up-and-into-the-net execution. A perfect play. The Canucks were still skating strong. There was absolutely no way that they could lose the game. Then memories of games gone by came to mind. Oh no, this is when the Canucks fold into a welcome mat and invite hulks to skate over them. John could feel his gut harden. They would just have to prove themselves.

John picked up his beer. "Who else could have been in on it?'

"Investors."

"The guys from New York?"

"Follow the money, that's what they say."

The game superseded John's interest in the money trail. Those final minutes were tense. The room was really noisy with guys shouting. Nothing is as much fun as your team winning. Carl was happy throughout the whole game but up until the last minute, a part of John expected Vancouver to lose somehow. He didn't have Carl's faith, at least not for the Canucks. Now, if it had been the Oilers playing, he would have believed. With the Canucks, he had to wait until the siren went. Then all of the tension left his body. The Canucks won. 3-2. Now they were up 2-1 in the Stanley Cup series of hockey heaven. It was a lot to absorb, but after the thrill wore off, he remembered that he hadn't heard the whole story.

"How'd Steve and Dan get away?" The place was still happy but not so loud anymore. Guys were serious about pool again.

"They were waiting in a clearing in the opposite direction from us. It's where they kept a stash of phony samples. We were all on the other side of a ridge, as Campbell knew well. The chopper picked them up after picking him up. We didn't see them. No one knew.

"The pilot ended up being the weak link in the chain. He was paid to fly and not talk to anyone about them. So what does he do? Right after they disappear, he quits work and starts drinking at the Tanzilla Pub in Dease Lake. Then he takes off for Hyder, Alaska, gets Hyderized, and ends up in jail. After that episode, he turns up in Stewart looking for work. This got back to the RCMP, who by then, wanted very much to talk to him anyway. That's how they found out about Steve and Dan. The pilot told the Mounties that he'd dropped them off in a clearing near Highway 37. They kept a truck there. They must have driven to Watson Lake or down to Prince George and got a plane out of the country to Mexico. That's where the Mounties said they went. They could have gone anywhere after that."

"That's some operation," said John. "Three guys plus the pilot in the field, along with the guys from back east raising the capital. Poof! It all disappears into an offshore account."

"Still a fly-by-night operation," said Carl. "They were small-minded crooks back in those days."

Those days are gone. Flying into Dease Lake now is flying into Tahltan territory. Mining executives have to bone up before meeting with the Chief in the Band Office in Telegraph Creek, after driving the scariest road in all of Canada, if not the world. Parts of the one-horse track are etched into the side of a four-hundred-foot canyon. The Tahltans never met Queen Victoria, didn't sign any treaties, never surrendered or ceded any of their land in the Cassiar to anyone, ever. Not in their history books. And standing in minus-thirty-degree temperatures, on a windy mountaintop overlooking the Grand Canyon of the Stikine, HMTQ is a long, long way away.

Carl and John sat quietly, thinking about fleecers and crooks. The bar was closing soon. The party was still on. The guys around the table next to them were still laughing, telling jokes, drinking beer, having a laugh.

Some people are always winging around the world, rich from their scams while everyone else plods along, thought John. That company dissolved since the mine was never going to materialize. These days, getting a mine going in the Cassiar will not happen without the cooperation of The People. John was working for Chief and Council.

They walked out of the American Hotel together and crossed Main Street, glancing up, without interest, at the broken neon sign. They climbed up the Georgia Viaduct to stand on the bridge, the city of Vancouver twinkling before them. They turned west to face Howe Street, the centre of their mining world, its tentacles reaching northward thousands of kilometres, all of the way to the Yukon border and beyond. Carl with stories of days past. John with stories still to come.

Murder on Main Street

Maybe if it had been an affair with a decent woman, she could have accepted it. If it had been someone like herself, only younger, attracted to him for his wealth and fine physique from a lifetime of healthy living. Why wasn't her husband seduced away by a pretty young woman, like a normal man? Or why not a younger man, even an older one, distinguished and charismatic? Instead, she was sitting in the cave-like Locus restaurant at Main and 25th, ensconced in the weird, exotic tree-roots decor, with lights dim and candles flickering, sipping on a divine coffee, waiting for a melt-in-your-mouth salad, trying to re-orient herself in her own life.

Monogamy. That was the deal. Infidelity was the deal-breaker. But this. What was this, after thirty years of marriage? She thought that they'd settled into a comfortable life. It wasn't like they hadn't gotten along. True, her expectations had never been met. Slowly, over the years, she had dreamed less often, less vividly, with less feeling, until she had stuffed her expectations into some closet in the back reaches of her unconsciousness. Cheerful acceptance had ruled her thoughts. Contentment of a sort had coloured her life. Now she looked back on the decades of her marriage with revulsion, revisiting all of her memories in the light of this new information, filtering them through a sordid lens to a new reality, her horror growing.

She hated him for his pretence, using her as a shield of respectability, transforming her into a domestic slave to a disgusting, filthy beast. He had cast her into this role without her knowledge or consent. The magnitude of the betrayal took her breath away. She thanked the heavens that they had never had children, their infertility now a blessing as well as a curse. Cold fury awakened in her. She looked around the darkened room as if it were inhabited by ghosts of women from bygone times. She could almost see poor Victorian spinsters sitting at the table next to her, their lives constrained to quiet desperation by their impoverished living standards while up in the window seats, the upper-class women, their bodies squashed by corsets, legs tied with yards of material and heads bound by wound-up tresses, stayed imprisoned by a life as chattel. She was no different. Nothing had really changed for her. She was caught in an old-fashioned marriage. She saw now how she'd given away her freedom in exchange for love and security, which had meant marriage. She saw now how it all went down, what women give and what they get in return.

    She sat amongst the ghosts of scorned women, betrayed women, of unloved women. Then she began to notice the ghosts of scheming women, manipulative women. The room was full of them. Women manoeuvre as best they can under patriarchal circumstances. It's only human. She thought of a story her grandmother had told her about how women used to kill their husbands. No thoughts of divorce, lawyers, documents, bank statements or shared assets crossed her mind. It all belonged to her. She was not going to share anymore. She was not going to care for him anymore. Instead, she would work with the overweight, out-of-shape, self-indulgent man that he was, unable to cook or clean for himself. He depended on her for everything, including all of his food. Well, ha ha, she thought. She had put unending energy into trying to curb his appetites to moderation. No more. She paid her bill, gathered up her shopping bags, and headed for Windsor Meats across the street.

    She looked at all of the organic beef and free-range happy chickens. She took some chicken burgers and a meat loaf. In a world gone to supermarket mediocrity, it was so reassuring that some fine traditions remained. Having a top-quality butcher and purveyor of local organic meat in her neighbourhood improved the quality of her life. She loved Windsor Meats. She loved Solly's too. His predilection for baked goods was going to be indulged with reckless abandon, starting with babkas on demand. She would buy six, along with four tubs of smoked-salmon cream cheese and a dozen bagels. He had never had a babka. It was a sensory delight she had kept him from experiencing for his own good or he'd have eaten two or three a day without a thought in his head. Now he could. She would make it possible for him to waft into Solly's legendary babka heaven without restraint. He was a goner, what with his weak will and willful ignorance.

She walked along Main Street, past the designer clothing stores where people came from all over the world to shop, so the magazines said. She thought it must be true because of late, she saw beautiful people on Main Street whom she could never have imagined walking past her back in the day. The street had changed so much since the days of true junk stores, used-car-part yards, and discount, mouldy food stores from 20th to 30th. You could date the beginning of the change from the time of Maurice's death in the early 1990s. He had owned a bunch of buildings along Main from 25th to 30th, one of which was a junk store filled to the ceiling with stuff. In good weather, he sat outside this store, chatting with everyone going by, never selling anything. After he passed on, his nephew sold all of the buildings. The junk store began to slowly empty, starting with the stuff that touched the ceiling. Things appeared on the sidewalk outside: lamps, fishing rods, lacrosse sticks, golf clubs, tables, and strange and fascinating knick-knacks. She had bought the very last thing he'd sold from that store, a wooden chair. She still had it in her hallway. Back then, there had been only a couple of restaurants around 25th. Now it was a foodie's paradise. Happily, she was a foodie.

She returned home and sat at her kitchen table, looking at the marble counter-tops, the oak cabinets, the tiled floor, the French doors, the outdoor living space. She surveyed her domain. She had sacrificed so much to accommodate a man not worth the effort. She had made a home for a weakling, a pathetic pervert who sat in front of a computer, titillating himself with pictures of reproductive organs, stimulating cranial nerves attached to the limbic system, the body's master of sex hormones and pleasure. Right-click, blood enters the spongy tissue. Discovering the internet porn had been a shock, of course. Like a mother discovering a Hustler under her son's mattress, she had tut-tutted and tsk-tsked in self-righteous anger and acceptance. Girlie magazines under the mattress, that's what she had thought that she was dealing with at first. What a quaint image from a bygone era, before the porn industry married digital media and spawned creatures hitherto unknown, unheard of, and unseen. Thinking that her husband had an internet porn problem had seared away at her respect, but she had still cared for him out of habit, if nothing else.

The porn discovery had motivated her to put a posturepedic bed in the guest room. She spun him a yarn about needing a special bed for the back problems that had plagued her all of her life. She rejoiced at the distance it put between them, never having to listen to him snore in her ear again. She truly regretted all of the lost sleep and clenched teeth, listening to the din pour forth from his engorged throat and bloated tongue.

The new matrimonial arrangement had seemed to brighten him up too. She had become suspicious, taking it upon herself to discover if there were duplicitous reasons for his uplifted mood. This had led her into new depths of his degradation. It had also led her to follow him to Main and Hastings in the middle of the night, then up Cordova to the industrial streets and parking lots by the docks, where she had watched her husband and a prostitute conduct business. They'd gone back down Cordova to Main. After he dropped her off, she'd pulled up to invite the woman into her car. Only it wasn't a woman. It was a child. A young girl, a frail, small child dressed up in tall spike heels, a tiny silver lame skirt, a tiny top, and tiny breasts pushed up over the edges of the scooped neckline. She had dried, dyed blonde hair around her tiny face, which was pockmarked and scabby, with sores on her thin hands. The anger that had roiled in her breast had choked her. She had almost fainted with a stabbing pity for the girl.

The poor, wretched child called herself Lady Ga Ga. More like Lady Gag Gag, she thought, listening to the poor mite talk about her husband, the john. She had thought about it the next morning when they went to church, his idea since they were married. She'd sat beside him, certainly not praying, but looking at him like he was one of those Mormons out at Bountiful pounding his fist on Holy Scripture proclaiming about

Moses, Moroni, obedience and his religious rights while a child bride sucks his dick. Oh, Jesus, Hallelujah.

As he sat in church, holding the hymn book, singing praises to the Lord, his balding head shone with sweat, his stubbly chinlets jiggled, and his burgeoning belly heaved. She thought that he was, no doubt, secretly singing to Lolita Dicklicker, his one true god. He had contaminated her mind. She looked away from him to observe the other men in the congregation, wondering how many of them used the church to protect their reputations and public image. Patriarchal religion, made by men for men, had turned women into domestic slaves, demonizing them in a creation story concocted by a bunch of old farts, sitting in their man-made deserts, getting fanned by slaves, counting their goats and wives. Good luck with that, she thought as she got up and left, never to go back.

She wondered how much of their money he spent secretly as if it were his money to spend on his porn and prostitute addiction. Ultimately, it was all pornography. Even a living, breathing girl was pornography to him. Her gut had wrenched, realizing with ever-deepening mortification and tortuous shame, that she was no more than a domestic slave blow-up doll to him. She was in a shell-marriage, a structure with no substance that she had accepted as her lot in life.

"Am I gaining weight?" he'd asked one night at dinner.

"No," she'd replied, dish cloth in hand, wiping down the counters.

"Oh," he'd said. "I guess not."

He'd left the room, not knowing that he'd eaten two thousand more calories than he needed at a sumptuous dinner: delectable stuffed pork chops baked in seasoned fat juices, organic potatoes mashed in mounds of rancid butter, and green beans sautéed at very high heat, all smothered in cheese sauce. On the side, he'd had a salad swimming in homemade mayonnaise, heavy on the eggs. She'd brought out the strawberry cream cakes from Breka's up on Fraser at 49th. While he watched TV, he'd consumed an additional twenty-five-hundred calories. The next day, he would wake up almost a kilo heavier. His heart would have to pump an additional one-hundred-and-sixty kilometres, and his arteries, already clogged, would bulge that much more from the pressure of the fatty deposits lining the walls. He would be that much closer to his inevitable end.

It was twisted, she knew. Buying new pants in a larger size. Carefully cutting the tags from the old smaller size to put into the new, much larger size. How would he know? He had never bought his own clothes, relying on her for all of his shopping. After all, he had said to her early on, he made more money. In his books, it was a pink job for her to do. At first, she'd been flattered that he loved her so much that he wanted her to take care of him, right down to the details of picking his clothes. Snow job. By the time she'd figured it out, it was too late.

"The belt never lies," he'd said all of his life. That was one of his little sayings when he looked down at his round tummy, which had been slowly growing over the years. Lately, the tummy was growing faster than ever. He was standing in front of the mirror, turning this way and that, possibly trying to fathom some niggling feeling.

"No, the belt never lies," she'd said in reply. His did. She'd taken great pains over the belt substitution, enlisting the help of Both Feet On Main Street, the shoe repair shop. The belt buckle was the same, but the belt was an exemplary display of fine craftsmanship.

"I don't need to weigh myself to know how I'm doing." Again, one of his foibles she counted on: his scales phobia. Before, she'd listened to the-belt-never-lies quip and thought, just step on the stupid scales and be done with it, but now she appreciated his little quirks.

"Very wise," she'd said. "You can't count on scales. You can weigh something different every day on the scales, but the belt never lies." She turned as she spoke so he wouldn't see her eyes rolling into the top of her head.

Where once she would have trumpeted an alarm at the rapid ballooning of his stomach, she now spoke lies with a deadpan face.

"You look the same," she'd said. "Are you worried? Do you want to go on a diet? Atkins maybe? I don't mind weighing your food." She turned back from the door to face him, innocent eyes looking at him with wifely concern, ignoring the fat wattle, the paunchy jowls, the distended belly, and the backside big as a barn.

He turned again, looking in the mirror. How was he to know the extraordinary effort she'd put into that mirror, not just any old mirror? It was made to elongate the figure in a flattering way, enhanced by a soft, gentle light above, which blurred edges into a pleasant surprise whenever anyone looked at themselves.

"I look fine," he'd said.

"You look great," she'd replied, averting her eyes from his grotesque body. She breathed into the hard knot in her heart, nurturing it, feeding it, caring for its presence, a rock-hard friend through long months of iron discipline. It was there for her when she was discovering the extent of his crimes against not only her, but all of humanity, including his own. Her heart was made of stone, giving her focus when she was counting calories, trans-fatty acids, and the high end of the glycemic index. Once she had cared, now she did not; her care switches were all turned to anti-care. All of the energy that she had put into keeping him healthy she now put into making him unhealthy. It was so easy. He couldn't have been a more willing victim.

When the end finally came, she was in the kitchen, scrubbing pots from the massive feast that she had produced for his dinner. It had featured mouth-watering, fat Maui ribs, dripping with her own sweet-and-sour pineapple sauce, heavy on the sweet. She had served this with fresh fettuccine from Granville Island Market and steamed Pemberton Valley potatoes, fried in old lard seasoned with freshly grated peppercorns. The Waldorf salad was heavy on the homemade mayonnaise that he was partial to, before he concluded with ice cream from the Gelato down near 12th and Main.

"Help, help."

She could hear the desperation in his voice, the pain, the fear. He was in the bathroom, but she could hear him just fine. She turned on the faucet full blast and leisurely rinsed a clean pot cleaner. He called her name. She rinsed another one and another one. She turned off the tap. She listened into the silence before making her way to the bathroom. She looked in. He was on the toilet. His pants were around his ankles. He was sweating, panting, weak, and paralyzed.

"Are you OK?" she'd asked.

"Phone 911," he'd said. Barely.

She'd stood there looking at him dispassionately. His eyes closed as his body contorted with a shudder. He was gone but still breathing. Then he was just gone, slumped into a toilet bowl, big, flabby, fat man. Slowly, he fell and sprawled onto the floor, his private parts a centrepiece in a fine display of natural death awaiting the paramedics.

She waited some respectful minutes for whatever may have been good about him to leave his body; it was only right. But her respect was fuelled by a sure and certain knowledge that he would burn in hell if there was one. It was almost worth believing in a patriarchal scare-mongering fairy tale in this life to enjoy the notion of his eternal suffering in the next.

She played the bereaved widow without much thought for the brief time that she appeared in public to mourn him. At home, in private, she reveled in her newfound freedom and self-esteem. She had rid the world of evil. She had done good. It made her feel good. Life was good, except for the memories of those poor, tortured children, selling their bodies for drugs. She sat at her kitchen table in her cozy home, surrounded by all of the things that she loved, her soft, warm hands clasped around a big mug of Grizzly Claw coffee. She wondered what those old grandmothers would have done if they had to contend with the digital age and these modern times that truly don't seem much different than times gone by.

She wondered if that street child Lady Ga Ga would like to sit in her kitchen, with the old, comfy, round oak table and chairs with ladybug seat covers. She could make the poor child some wholesome food and begin to care again. Caring, her true nature, had been exploited and misused. She imagined Lady Ga Ga lying in her husband's bed, since she herself was never going to live in that room again. Maybe Lady Ga Ga could use a nice bed. It was the least a child could expect from life, a nice bed in a nice house, safe from all of the predators. She took a deep breath and imagined cooking delightful meals for the abused-children-turned-drug-addicts wandering downtown, hurt, rejected, and frightened. She'd be doing something heartfelt, have a focus for her love of life, and for her profound gratitude for her release from a domestic prison. She still had all of her best years ahead.

Women Watching on Main Street

Someone was digging in the Skinny Bin dumpster parked in the lane beside the YWCA on Hornby Street. Grace could hear scrabbling noises and rumbling sounds as garbage was tossed around. She was watching, waiting to see who was inside, when up to the bin biked a young guy wearing a yellow jacket, one of those seriously outdoors, thick, waterproof-yellow jackets. He stopped at the bin and began talking to it, but she was too far away to actually hear him.

She was sitting on the low retaining wall outside the Y, cooling off after her kilometre of front crawl in the Y's ozonated pool, then a muscle-relaxing dip in the hot tub, followed by a detoxifying steam bath. Soon she'd hop on her bike to ride up the steep, grinding hill from 2nd to 25th, along the Ontario bike route that ran next to Main Street. She'd get in another good workout before arriving home to her comfy house. She loved her bike ride to and from work.

Grace lived in a cozy heritage house on top of South Hill at Main and 37th, with its spectacular views of the North Shore mountains, Burnaby Mountain, the Burrard Inlet, and sometimes, Mt. Baker, Washington. For three years, she'd come home from working in an office all day, only to spend the evening working on a reno. Weekends too. Now it was a beautiful house and only five kilometres from her office on Howe Street. Sweet.

She lost interest in the bin turning to look upward at the stained-glass windows of the sumptuous hotel across the little laneway, all orange and golds, warm and cheery. Behind her, written in a metre high blue letters on the Y building wall was the sign: Find Your Balance. She certainly thought that she'd found hers.

The guy on the bike at the bin started to come towards her so she turned to look at him. Behind his back, a head popped up like a prairie dog from inside the bin, swivelling right and left. A woman's head, and boy, oh boy, was she ugly. Hugely ugly. It was hard to imagine anyone looking worse. She had lank, greasy tendrils of rat's tails hanging from her head, possibly once-was-hair. Her skin was sallow and hanging with jaundiced fatigue, her lips thin and sunken, her cheeks collapsed inward, her teeth dark and missing. This made her open mouth look like a black hole in a white porcelain sink, stained yellow. Her eyes were sunken into her skull, her forehead short and sloping. Ugly. Gulping ugly. She could not have made herself more ugly. She was beautifully, perfectly ugly. If ugly is invisible, she was never ever seen.

In a fluid movement, she slithered out of the bin. She was tall and very, very thin, wearing a dark, shapeless coat, unbuttoned, baggy, blue pants and a dark green, shapeless sweater, hanging to her knees. All of her winter clothing blended into the shadows, her fashion statement more invisibility. Funnily enough, she was on roller blades, a Wiley Coyote stick woman with giant feet, circling around, holding up a LuluLemon shopping bag like it was the Olympic torch. Score. Then she disappeared, skating off into the shadows.

Biker guy pedalled over to Grace, smiling. "I could kick her out but there isn't much point. If I treat her kindly, then she tells me stuff. No one knows what's going on more than people like her. So I'm nice to her, she's nice to me, and I always know what's going on." He laughed.

"Yeah. Why be mean when it's nicer to be nice." She smiled back at him.

"But it's a choice," he said. "They should get jobs."

"Doing what?" she replied. She'd heard this one before. "You think she could do your job? Show me a business that wants to lose money employing traumatized people. It's some choice to be mentally ill and addicted to pharma-medicine concocted by FAS half-wits and psychopaths playing quasi-chemists in unsanitary, homemade, duct-taped laboratories."

He leaned closer and focused his face more towards her, curious. "Well, that's true, for some people," he replied. "But they should get help then."

He was beginning to hunker down into a more serious tone. She said, "What I find strange is that the saddest people terrorize us with their petty crimes. We're always being victimized by victims."

She paused as they noticed a sleek black car pulling into the alleyway, wanting to park. Biker guy became distracted from her pithy wisdom as he blocked the car. It came to a stop.

"For such a small group of people, they sure play havoc on our lives." Biker guy had gotten in front of the car, gearing up for something other than casual blather.

"You can't park here," he said to the guy behind the wheel. He walked to the passenger side as the guy rolled down the window.

She leaned down to get a look at the driver. He had a small head, relatively speaking. Maybe because it was shaved bald. She could see a stubble shadow on part of his tight skull. His face pulled back in a sneer. She wondered if he had a hairy back.

In the meantime, Biker guy was getting assertive. "Sorry. No parking here. You can go right through the alley to Dunsmuir Street. You don't need to turn around."

"What?" said the driver. "I park here all the time. Look, I forgot my pass."

"There are no passes that can let you park here," replied Biker guy.

"Look, you go in there and ask for Gus." He pointed at the Y doors. Gus was probably in there working out his triceps and pumping his pecs.

"Gus cannot give you permission to park here. It is a no parking zone." Biker guy was getting frustrated. So was the driver. It looked to her like he was one of those little-wienie type of guys.

"Go in there and talk to Gus," shouted Little Wienie.

"You can't park here. Period. Gus or no." Biker guy was not shouting per se, but his voice was definitely tinged with assurance and authority.

Little Wienie craned his neck even further from his shoulders, trying to get a better angle out the passenger window for what was rapidly descending into a confrontation. "I forgot my pass, now let me park." His shout didn't really have the force he was looking for. You can't strain your neck trying to poke it out as far as it will go and retain all your dignity, especially if throbbing veins are blinking in your forehead. And it must affect your speech muscles because the little guy was pretty much incomprehensible. "Get blip blop me moo blu blah or I will blimp blab bork you blob."

Little Wienie finally realized that he was going to need more of a purchase, so to speak, to make his assault, leaning over as he was, shouting at Biker guy's crotch, so he rolled up the window and sped away in obvious disgust. Defeated.

Biker guy looked over his shoulder at her. They looked at each other, smiled, and both shrugged. She was sitting with her legs crossed, elbow on her knee, her chin resting on her upturned hand. She raised her eyebrows at him.

"You wouldn't believe," he said. And just then, she saw a movement in the shadows. She turned to look up the alleyway and saw the sporty little car heading back towards them. Little Wienie hadn't really gone away. Instead of driving through to Dunsmuir while taking a philosophical view of life and parking scams, he'd gone up the alley and managed to turn around, so that he could roar back, roll down his window, and shout at Biker guy without having to crane his neck.

"You're nothing," he screamed at Biker guy, his complexion turning an apoplectic shade. "Who are you? You're a parking attendant, that's all you are. You're nothing. Nothing. All you can do is be a parking attendant. Who are you to stop me anyway?"

Obviously, Little Wienie didn't see ambulances and fire trucks the way the rest of us do. No social contract, civic agreement, intelligent plan for living together. Nobody gets to park in the emergency vehicle lane ways. Righty-ho, say we. Not me, says he. And more to the point, he wasn't up on the who's who of privilege when it comes to Main Street, Vancouver.

As everyone on Main Street knows, biking jackets exude certain messages. Yellow rain jackets like the one worn by Biker guy of good, solid military issue, devoid of anything written on them, especially "Security," speak volumes. Rain gear from MEC – say no more. Value Village Boutique – young woman, city bike. Then there are the particularities of the waterproof jerseys of the high-flying racer-guys. Much time can be spent quantifying and qualifying the biker rain jackets of Main Street.

"You're at the bottom riding a bicycle," shouted the Little Wienie. "You're scum." She looked at the bike. It had "Specialized" written on the frame. Bottom indeed. She leaned forward to see if he had the Dynamite 3000 titanium seat suspension while the tirade continued.

"You're just a loser parking attendant."

This finally got Biker guy's goat. Like on TV, he whipped out a wallet with a flick of the wrist, flip-flop, revealing his badge of power and authority to stop abusive shaved-bald guys from doing anti-social things. It took a minute of graceless grumbling and let-me-see-that mumbling, but finally Little Wienie realized he'd been trumped with a Go-Straight-To-Jail card. He sped off with excruciatingly predictable car-groaning histrionics. Biker guy turned to her and said with fierce determination, "I'm going to make sure he doesn't park illegally on the street," before jumping on his bike to pedal furiously out of the alley, turning left down Hornby.

"You do that," she called after him. "Here's to you," she thought.

Movement caught her eye. Twirling Girl emerged from the shadows, her lank tendrils falling over her grey face. "The guy in the car's a jerk," she said. She twirled closer.

Grace took her elbows off her knees and sat up straight on the low wall to face her. "Totally mean." She held up her thumb and index finger in the little wienie sign. "I hate guys like that."

Twirling Girl made the hand sign too as she twirled closer, throwing back the tendrils, showing her scarred face. "There's lots of guys just like that. You wouldn't believe how many guys I've met like that. I've been beaten up so many times by those kind of guys. They're everywhere. They're the worst."

She twirled slowly in a circle, and then another, spiralling. Suddenly smiling, she became a young woman with light flickering in her eyes. Then she quickly skated off down the alley to be swallowed up into the shadows.

www.ingramcontent.com/pod-product-compliance
Lightning Source LLC
Chambersburg PA
CBHW032133090426
42743CB00007B/580